Tin Barn
Philosopher

Wolf DeVoon

ISBN 978-0-359-37310-9

DEAR READER

Thank you for trusting me.

I try to get the facts straight, with less than perfect results. The writing is often cruel and offensive. It's important to post a review, to speak your mind in reply, especially if you believe that I got something completely wrong.

As a free people, we have enormous opportunities in life.

One of our most cherished freedoms in America is the right of free speech. It can be abused. Some of what I think and say may be interpreted as hate speech. I don't actually feel that about anyone. The struggle for life compels people of every race, sexual orientation, experience and circumstance to take action as they must, including those who support or benefit from coercive government and taxation.

It has been my life purpose to quarrel with that, to express my conviction that liberty is best, however messy it often seems. It must be defended vigorously, with civilian police, military power, and common law justice — none of which was available to colonial Americans. They were ruled by a corrupt Parliament, royal courts, and redcoats who fought overseas wars in fealty to rapacious ministers of state.

Subject Index

The Ugly Side of Anarchy

Conservatives are alternately disgusted and worried about young "anarchists" throwing rocks at cops in Berkeley and Portland. That's small potatoes, not a big problem.

The narcotics threat is infinitely worse. It took a strike force of 600 Feds and local crime units to round up 60 hard guys who were paid-up members of the East Coast Crips network, most of them wanted for serious felonies, connected to a NY prison gang. Multiply that by 20 states minimum, thousands of killers still at large, coast to coast. Add MS-13 and five or six Mexican cartels. There may be as many as 100,000 dangerous men on our streets, armed to the teeth, cash flow positive from drug dealing. They have a million retail customers, each of whom has to commit petty crime to fix an addict's craving to get high, or at least stave off the nightmare of withdrawl another day or two. Maybe another million are involved in the meth scene and widely-prescribed pharmaceutical opiates, some reckless morons using both.

It's difficult to estimate the number of Americans who smoke pot, maybe 20 million. These geriatric gentlefolk are easy meat for the DEA, but harder to find and not much of a public threat. Ditto millions of drunks, most of whom are employed, driving buzzed and texting a pal for laughs. Add them all together — hardened gangsters and addled dopes — it's perhaps 33 million (10% of U.S. population) on the wrong side of criminal law and sobriety. The impact on women and children is horrible. They suffer grievous harm financially, psychologically, and often physically. Many are destined to become permanent wards of the state.

Sorry, that's not the BIG problem, however awful drug and alcohol abuse are.

We're dumbing down the next generation at an alarming rate, a combination of "education" in American schools and endless waves of obscenity in our mass media, digital connectivity, and propaganda emanating from public servants and political operatives. Many tens of millions have been hosed with hate. Their children are being raised with the conviction that America is fundamentally evil, by reason of our (somewhat) free market in finance and (somewhat) splendid military strength. Folks are apt to over-estimate how strong we are in reality. Seven of our ten aircraft carrier strike groups are in port for repairs. The Air Force is flying antique fighters and tankers. We need replacement equipment and new recruits for a U.S. Army that did too much with too little money. There are never enough Marines.

Americans are confused about who's doing what to who, specifically with respect to politics and retail democracy. Foreign powers have little impact on us. Hollywood and New York are homegrown threats to the general welfare and domestic tranquility, broadcasting evil day and night, 24/7/365. It doesn't matter whether the sauce de jour is Donald Trump, or a college sport gab fest, or the latest excuse to get high on big screen "entertainment," or crime news, sanitized to conceal a one-sided race war that's decidedly obvious and that no one wants to discuss. Much easier to feel wronged by law enforcement, courageous people who put their lives on the line to defend us, an increasingly impossible duty. It escapes notice that cops are hamstrung by paperwork and due process, spend much of their time testifying in court after a lonely shift answering calls for domestic battery, directing traffic around a car accident, while deeply worried about stopping a stolen car because odds are they'll have to kill or be killed. The life of an LEO is nonstop horror and boredom, dealing with drunks and dead babies, gang wars, lunatics, theft, shoplifting, fistfights, stabbings, and noise complaints.

It's important to understand that cops and U.S. military are few, about two million — vastly outnumbered by bureaucrats, government contractors, public school teachers, doctors and nurses poorly compensated by Medicaid, Medicare, and VA appropriations. We have more postal workers than cops, a larger army of municipal garbage collectors and janitors than soldiers and sailors and airmen. Public service comprises about 40% of economic activity, if you count all the

IT people involved in making government more complicated and expensive than it otherwise might be.

Does all this government achieve anything?

Yes and no. Compliance with regulations and tax accounting kills American jobs, makes us dependent on China for cheap goods, reliant on imported oil and foreign bondholders. It's nice to be "the cleanest dirty shirt" of global finance, to cover our endless stream of public borrowing and government largesse. As goofy as it sounds, U.S. Treasury instruments are considered good collateral that can be rehypothecated and leveraged, employing thousands of traders who get to skim a nice seven-figure annual income, come what may, from "dark pools" of derivatives estimated at $1 quadrillion in notional value. Hard to grasp that it's all built on Treasury debt that cannot be retired and keeps growing in size, not including our unfunded entitlement problem and a hopelessly bloated Federal Reserve balance sheet.

The positive aspect of fat U.S. federal, state, and local spending is an illusion of Normalcy, some success in assuring the American people that cops and firemen will respond when you need them to clean up a relatively small tragedy. National Guard part-time citizen soldiers can be deployed to deal with big problems, hurricane, flood, or race riots. The government is ready to handle a lot of pain, albeit too little too late to save anyone's life or property.

Does it make sense to spend 40% of our productive output on government? Oops, wrong question. It's a fiction of economic theory that government spending is a component of notional Gross Domestic Product. In reality, the private sector (60% of GDP) is 100% of our productive output — and even that's exaggerated by incomes paid to finance, insurance, and real estate scalpers. So, productive work struggles to carry the "sterile" half of GDP — and fails to cover the total cost of lavish bureaucracy and entitlement payola. That's why government has to be deficit financed, more and more debt each fiscal year. States and localities are caught in the same trap, no way out. Higher taxes woud kill job creation, put more people out of work.

All perfectly dire, no way to turn back the clock and put government on a diet. However that's not the worst of our troubles. American liberty (anarchy) is a widely spread fabric of American culture, shared by federal, state, and local government workers, because they too are private citizens just like us, determined to be as free as possible in the direction of their lives, who to marry, which home to buy, how to feed and clothe and amuse their kids. They get sick, visit the doctor, attend churches and support charities, mow the lawn, no different than anyone else. Working for a government agency doesn't make someone less anarchist or more responsible at home. They drink. They watch TV and binge on chili cheese nachos.

The fundamental problem with American anarchy, all of it, from career criminals to the cops who try to stop bad guys, is our universal displeasure in facing facts. We became addicted to flattery, brainless amusements, and sleepy indifference to American history.

Let's discuss flattery first. Did you invent iron smelting, steel-making, internal combustion, interchangeable parts, mass production, fractional distillation, and ten thousand other ideas that put an affordable vehicle in your driveway? — nope.

Did you invent radio, television, semiconductors, digital processors, packet switching, or liquid crystals? — nope.

Most of the stuff we use in daily life was an international effort involving basic science and industrial technology that evolved over centuries of trial and error, capitalism, competition, and wars for possession of raw material, especially oil, rubber, copper, bauxite, magnesium, nickel, zinc, titanium, etc. Wars were fought over food and water, fruit, transportation corridors, religions, and something as stupid as animal pelts. You stand on the shoulders and buried corpses of hundreds of millions of warriors, thousands of scientists, tens of thousands of crackpot inventors and ruthless stock market frauds. It's still happening today, stock market manipulation in particular. Pensions and individual investors are going to be kneecapped again, depend on it. There is a quiet trade war underway for scarce rare earth metals. Your individual contribution to prosperity is zero, no matter what your job, and the purchasing power of a buck is subject to change without notice. Not that long ago a "buck" was the skin of a male deer.

Doe skins were half a buck. Could you feed yourself without grocery stores, mechanized agriculture, imported oil? Don't flatter yourself.

Brainless amusements are so thoroughly familiar and comfy that it's almost impossible to imagine life without pro sports, movies, TV, digital games, smart phones, and social media. None of it is necessary (like food and water and sanitation are). None of it makes you any smarter or wiser. Without advertising, it all collapses, and advertising is the first thing to go in a deep recession. Same thing with higher education. A degree in sociology or urban planning is worthless if the public purse snaps shut. Folks have lost sight of what the "business cycle" and "reversion to the mean" imply for discretionary spending on Star Trek conventions, binge viewing, multiplayer fantasy warfare, gay nightclubs, and elective cosmetic surgery. You are one paycheck from losing that leased Camaro or F-150. Government jobs have a little more security, but fun and games vanish for everybody in a deep recession.

That's why American history matters. We're living in an era very similar to the Roaring 20s, or rather at the end of it, fantastically in-flated market values. Uber has never made a penny of profit, and they burned through $4 billion. Same thing with Amazon, a microscopic margin, loaded with unpayable debt. Ditto shale drillers, automobile manufacturers, airlines, casual dining, department stores, malls and specialty retailers. Most gasoline stations are independently owned no matter what the sign says in front, and they squeak by on convenience store sales of cold beer, overpriced potato chips, cigarettes, lottery tickets, and watery fountain drinks. A big dip in sales (or a flash mob of looters) would be enough to shut their doors and turn off the gas pumps, lay off the minimum wage staff. Same thing at McDonald's and Burger King, barely profitable with bargain menus during boom times, unsustainable in a crash.

The last time we had a serious recession was NOT in living memory, unless you're 100 years old, which means you were 11 or 12 years old when the market crashed in 1929, old enough to understand and remember. For the rest of us, it's a question of American history. The crash was an overture to ten years of truly awful widespread poverty and hunger. Maybe we're in a different situation today? — maybe —

but I'll remind you that the Great Depression was the cause of world war, which sounds particular terrifying today because so many nutso dictatorships have (or can easily obtain) nuclear weapons.

So. The ugly side of anarchy is not so much what might happen next, but rather how we got ourselves into this mess. Americans voted for bread and circuses. No one forced it on you. We became accustomed to the best of everything, available for the asking. You don't even have to work at a job. Crime pays. Social Security pays and Medicare pays. SNAP and welfare benefits pay. I hope you know that 2/3 of federal spending is mandatory "entitlements" that can't be cut without public outrage, instantly voting into office a socialist Congress to spend and borrow our way back to the American Daydream in defiance of reality — because a bad recession at home means economic disasters abroad. Foreign bondholders will cash in their enormous stack of Treasury bonds, while we're trying to sell more. It's a solid concrete barrier to sustained or increased domestic spending to fend off pain during a recession.

What to do about it is simple. Use your liberty to prepare, and for heaven's sake please stop watching television and bitching about Donald Trump. He had nothing to do with LBJ's Great Society, Carter's Community Redevelopment Act, or Obamacare and expanded Medicaid. It's likely that a crisis would bring another silver-tongued FDR to power, so watch out for bank holidays and public works programs, defunding military strength and readiness.

And worse, the 1930s multiplied gangsters, armed with machine guns, paying graft to cops and Democrat political bosses. Bad idea to relocate to Chicago or Philadelphia now. Detroit is already destroyed. Baltimore is next, no crisis required, and I worry about Newark, Queens, Brooklyn, and Los Angeles.

War with Iran is a bad idea

A few days after the 9/11 WTC and Pentagon attacks, the FBI identified all 19 hijackers. Fifteen of the men were from Saudi Arabia. So, why didn't we bomb Saudi Arabia?... Saddam Hussein had absolutely nothing to do with 9/11. So, why did we invade and occupy Iraq at a cost of $2 trillion and 4,400 dead? — not counting 1.8 million refugees and 100,000 Iraqi dead. In 2005, a Pentagon study found that one in four U.S. troops who survived the Iraq War came home with health problems that required medical or mental health treatment, over 79,000 casualties. (CONSTITUTION OF GOVERNMENT IN GALT'S GULCH, P. 139)

I was surprised to discover that Objectivists led by Yaron Brook are stumping for war, this time to attack Iran — and if I understand it correctly, they counsel "total war" on Iran as a cure for terrorism. Both propositions are absurd.

We aren't prepared to attack anyone with conventional weapons and U.S. troops, a widely known fact. There are thousands of jihadis in England and America who will strike back. Terrorism would increase in scale and scope. Iran is allied with Russia. Use of tactical nukes to make up for troop shortfalls and mothballed A-10s could trigger intercontinental nuclear war. The Russians built underground shelters for their entire civilian population. We have none, aside from a couple bunkers in Virgina for high-ranking officials, to provide continuity of U.S. government. On 9/11, Vice President Cheney was whisked into one of the "secure locations," while George W. boarded a special 747 equipped for communications with our strategic forces worldwide, including submerged nuclear submarines.

But, okay, let's suppose that conventional U.S. military strength and readiness for war could be rebuilt in relatively short order, perhaps five or six years. It's possible that propaganda might rally Congressional and popular support. It remains, however, that fighting a war with Iran will be no easier than Iraq. I think the butcher's bill could be much higher, because Iran has modern air defenses. It's conceivable that front line Russian fighters have been secretly pledged to assist Iran in case of attack. Russian bombers overflew Iran to hit Syria.

Let's suppose further that Saudi Arabia and Israel will help us, re-enacting the sequence of blunders that spawned Al-Qaeda, led by Osama bin Ladin. His 1996 fatwah condemned U.S. forces being based on the "holy" Arabian Peninsula which includes Bahrain, 5th Fleet base in the Persian Gulf. I think it's preposterous to assume that killing bin Ladin ended dissent. ISIS is operational in Libya; another U.S. war in the Middle East could destabilize Egypt.

What's the point of taking the Sunni side in war against Shi'ites? What outcome is desired? Occupation of Iraq did not eliminate sectarian loyalty or prayers five times a day. The instant we withdrew, it all went to hell. Or is that the goal? Vengeful wrath, destruction of Iran for what unforgivable crime exactly? I can understand that Israel feels threatened and wronged, but centuries-old Middle East feuds have nothing to do with defending the United States.

> *I don't see any justification for overseas adventures. Israel can fend for itself, unless they wish to apply for admission to the Union, which would entitle them to the protection of the United States, no different than Idaho or New Jersey.* (LAISSEZ FAIRE LAW, P. 2)

Trump's new alliance with Saudi Arabia is particularly bizarre. It's a totalitarian monarchy with religious police. Women are treated like chattel. I spent three months in Libya and had ample opportunity to observe the status of females in an Islamic country. You cannot free anyone by aiding fundamentalist Wahhabi tyranny.

Fess up. Is this, in fact, about oil?

I hope not. Saudi oil reserves are shrinking. The Export Land Model accurately predicted that they would consume more each year domestically for power generation and desalinisation. Qatar and Saudi Arabia are eager to ship natural gas to Europe, which is why they support mercenary proxies in Syria, hoping to build a pipeline through Syria, understood and assisted by the Obama Administration State Department and "Other Government Agencies."

I've had some experience with OGAs. They derive a sick sense of purpose, pride, and pleasure inflicting cruelty. But let's put that miserable business aside. War is something that DoD does.

With Iran in ruins, Saudis and Qataris would be enabled to exploit the entire offshore Gulf gas play, unless Russia has a motive to stop them (which they do). Whether Germany remains a Gazprom customer or not, I fail to see what the United States gains from a war to rearrange the international market for gas. The United States is amply supplied with domestic natural gas. With very little effort we could produce more from conventional fields and shale.

Not true of oil. Another reason to suspect that war with Iran will echo war in Iraq. The Cheney Energy Commission recommended invasion of Iraq to gain control of its southern reserves, long before 9/11. I saw the documents. If Bremer's imperium had maintained control, U.S. majors were ready bid for production licenses and commit billions to grow proved reserves. Since the mid-70s, all Western oil companies have been desperate to add conventional oil reserves. Acquisition of shale gas production was predicated on a laughable accounting fraud, booking gas as "oil equivalent." Tillerson admitted that Exxon hasn't made a penny of profit from its shale acquisitions. The price of natural gas fell from $10 to $2 mcf, and gas is NOT oil.

The United States imports about a third of its oil supply, and with Venezuela about to die as an oil producer, I can understand strategic alliance with Saudi Arabia, weapons sales, making a gesture (special forces sent to Yemen) to advance our interest as an oil importer. Aramco employs a lot of U.S. citizens, in both Saudi Arabia and the Gulf of Mexico. It's a comfortable deal, but decidedly not worth fighting for, if it means total war to destroy and lay waste to Iranian oil production.

We do not win anything by reducing world oil supplies.

Or is that the purpose? — to cripple Iranian oil production, cut off financial support for Hamas and Hezbollah? If so, then we should be honest about it, that the purpose of U.S. "total war" against Iran is to advance the interests of Israel. I don't think We The People will agree to pay another $2 trillion and suffer tens of thousands of "wounded warrior" tragedies in fealty to Israel again, after being tricked into doing it once before in 2003.

Donald Trump was elected to keep us out of the Middle East, make peaceful overtures to Russia, not to start a war.

I can understand Trump's conversion to the Neo-con faith. It's sobering to take office as the Commander-In-Chief, and he's under tremendous pressure to disprove "collusion" with our historic super-power rival. War with Russia's ally Iran is taking things a bit too far, likely to end the Trump presidency in total, immediate failure, from the moment he tweets war as a policy objective. Tough talk is fine. But actually preparing for war with Iran would toss him out of office in 2020, and midterm Congressional elections will halt appropriations to equip the U.S. Army, Navy, Air Force, and Marines for massed expeditionary combat.

If there is a conversation to be had about war with Iran, it should be a conspiracy to flummox the American electorate, scare the shit out of them again, a shocking nuclear weapon threat with dastardly Russian and North Korean "collusion." It would be helpful to plant a few false flag stories staged for the press. Satellite reconnaisance, arrival of a mysterious cargo ship or MH 370 repainted in camo.

Reality check

A comment on Facebook got my attention and deserves more discussion, as to whether the U.S. can cut all foreign aid, produce our own renewable energy, and screw OPEC. Let's talk about energy first. "Renewable" means solar, wind, hydro, and nuclear. All of it is expensive to install and maintain. None of it can power a meaningful fraction of our transportation and heavy equipment like tractors, bulldozers, big rigs, jet aircraft, barge tugs, or electric power generation. The fuel of choice nowadays is natural gas. We have enough to keep the lights on in New York and run some buses and urban delivery vans — but that's all. There's not enough gas in the ground to power our entire fleet of passenger cars and pickup trucks, period.

Experiments with LNG-powered big rigs were a flop, and you can forget about LNG-powered aircraft or heavy equipment. Diesel and kerosene are a permanent part of our energy future, unless you propose to halt air traffic and construction. Our military runs on vast supplies of diesel, gasoline, and jet fuel. We need oil — a lot of it — unless you want to drag your family back to the Middle Ages, close all of our hospitals, farms and factories, forego all plastics in packaging, plumbing and electric wiring, all fertilizers, asphalt, lubricants, and buckets.

I've been an oil patch analyst for 15 years. Unconventional fracking is a losing proposition, about $80 billion in debt. There are very few plays that are profitable at today's price of $50 bbl. Bakken isn't one of them. Nor are Canadian tar sands, gas-to-liquids conversion, or blue-green algae. Our main resources are deepwater Gulf of Mexico, California, and the Rockies. None of it is cheap, but it beats the pants off squeezing oil out of tight shale formations. There are no new oil discoveries to be found in North America. Prudhoe Bay is very nearly exhausted.

Our allies are in worse shape than we are. The North Sea has been drilled to death. Norway is exploring the Arctic. There's some potential offshore Newfoundland and Greenland, but it's costly and difficult. Brazil is pulling its hair out, attempting to fracture the pre-salt play. Our industrial allies Germany, Japan and South Korea have no oil, period. They depend entirely on shipments of imported oil and LNG, most of it from the Middle East and Africa. If Mexico and Venezuela collapse, which is increasingly likely, we'll join the club of oil beggars, trying to out-bid China, India, the Asian Tigers, and Europe (3 billion people) for scarce supplies.

Russia, Saudi Arabia, Qatar, Kuwait, Iraq and Iran have 3/4 of the world's remaining crude oil and natural gas reserves — a natural endowment with very low extraction cost. Historically, the U.S. and Britain were instrumental in developing all of those resources. We bankrolled governments and did most of the frontier geology and drilling two generations ago. France, Germany, Italy, and Holland spent huge sums in Africa and SE Asia. World War II was a global war for oil in the Caspian, Indonesia, and Persia. Recently we gave Russia tens of billions for joint venture projects and got screwed, almost nothing to show for it. Same thing happened to Royal Dutch Shell in Mexico, Conoco and Exxon in Venezuela, Standard Oil in Saudi Arabia.

It sounds crazy, but North Korea isn't a strategic threat, nor the nuclear weapons in Pakistan and India, Israel and Iran (soon enough). The great problem worldwide is oil. That's why we have hundreds of military bases, guided missile cruisers and carrier battle groups around the globe, to keep sea lanes open, supertankers shuttling from the Persian Gulf and third world hellholes like Nigeria, to oil-starved Japan, Korea, Germany, China, and U.S.A.

Not much doubt that we're overstretched and made terribly costly blunders like invading Iraq, ultimately handing its rich Southern oil fields to Shi'ites aligned with Iran, our tanks and small arms captured by lunatic Sunni renegades that became ISIS, backed by Saudi money — our "ally" the pious Wahhabi fundamentalists who attacked us on 9/11 and blamed Taliban tribesmen that we armed to fight the Soviets.

I can't think of one thing America did right in Arabia. We backed Pavlavi and lost Iran. We backed Assad and then abandoned him, let ISIS seize his oil fields and sell oil to NATO "ally" Erdogan who shipped it to Israel, another "ally" who pried the Kurds away from Baghdad and got U.S. covert support for a Libyan bloodbath that forged a Russian-Iranian alliance. Brilliant, huh? We have 50,000 U.S. troops in Kuwait, Qatar and Bahrain, smack in the middle of a crossfire between Arabia and Iran when it comes to war, as it most assuredly must. Blockade of Qatar is an overture to something far worse, and Trump opened Raytheon's war chest on credit, because the Saudis are bankrupt.

How one of the world's largest oil producers could be upside-down financially is simple. We did it, too, $20 trillion in unpayable U.S. debt, spending too much on domestic entitlements and payola to our "allies" in Western Europe, Middle East, and Pacific Rim. Russia is in the same fix, despite big cash flow selling oil and natural gas to Western Europe and China. Cost of extraction and graft eats up profit, and U.S./UK majors are disinclined to get screwed again, no matter what Putin offers them. War risk is hot on everyone's front burner — except the rump American middle class, preoccupied with the price of a college education and whether Wall Street can notch another improbable gain before the market crashes.

Reality checks are no fun. $50 oil is starvation for U.S. frackers, for Canadian tar sands, Russian playboys, and jewel-encrusted ragheads. That's why they're ready for war, to goose the price of oil to $100 or more.

Good idea to get our boys out of harm's way, say fuck it, you're on your own in Afghanistan, Arabia, the Magreb, Western Europe, Japan, Korea, and Israel. Probably take years to wind down overseas bases, won't save a penny because it's expensive to retire a granfalloon.

Go ahead call a cop

L. Neil Smith posts thought pieces from time to time on Facebook, and I started following him as a Facebook "friend." I did likewise with tech wizard Tom Lahti, Pierre Lemieux, and Ilana Mercer, although in Ilana's case she's such a strikingly stunning vamp that it was a no-brainer. I have a weak spot for the fair sex, especially when they're tough, courageous, beautiful, and have jet black hair like Lt. Janet DiMarco, one of my very favorite fictional creations.

Well, yesterday L. Neil opined that a wall to seal off the U.S. border was a good idea, and it elicited a variety of comments, including mine. I said that as a matter of legal principle there have to be public roads to get from Point A to Point B, and that the Right of Liberty coupled with a presumption of innocence precludes shutting anyone out of the U.S. with a wall. That intersects the public outcry about keeping people from boarding airplanes and an equally hot debate about "sanctuary cities" that flout complicated Federal immigration statutes.

I'm not a big fan of legislation. I have yet to discover anything that Congress ever did to the betterment of the Republic. We're hopelessly bankrupt, our military is overstretched and underfunded, money has poured into the stock market thanks to financial repression (zero interest paid on savings), and "mandatory" entitlements are ironclad largesse that Democrats and Republicans swear hand on heart in unison shall be law forever — a perpetual flood of borrowed money to pay for Social Security, Medicare, Medicaid, Food Stamps, free housing for millions of single moms and their nurseries of future gangsters and drug addicts, a wide delta of subsidies and grants for education, solar energy, electric cars, corn ethanol, public works, FEMA payola, etc. I don't know if anyone can compile a comprehensive list of Federal and state handouts. Most mortgages are backed by GSE paper, exempting banks and brokers from lending risk, and bank deposits are guaranteed by FDIC that will be exhausted instantly in a panic.

If I understand it correctly, Federal tax law provides a cash "refund" if someone has little or no income and paid no tax. I should look into that.

Of course, orthodox Objectivists condemn taking money from government, the unearned, the worst of all possible evils. One of the O'ist holy rollers on Facebook jumped all over me for saying that Liberty trumped property. He claimed he had an inherent Right to Life that translated into absolute dominion of his property, and every inch of dirt everywhere should be privately owned. He didn't know that Wolf DeVoon said the same thing repeatedly, with the caveat that property rights are limited by what the neighbors will allow. I didn't explain who I was. I poked him in the jugular:

<< *Don't be silly. There is no natural right to life or anything else. Your birth was an involuntary dice roll, your early years a gift from parents who owed their prosperity to benefactors who bequeathed an industrial society not of your making. Now you come along and assert that you OWN something, to the exclusion of everyone else's liberty and their putative equal right to life. You want it both ways, an absolute right to your life, denial of liberty belonging to others. Go ahead, call a cop, demand protection. What you'll find is that your neighbors will vote your ass outta there with property taxes, public roads, zoning, building codes, and settlement of refugees next door. A is indeed A.* >>

The Randian promptly went ballistic. If there's no objective morality, then you could rape children, nothing would be right or wrong, and how dare I cite the sacred Law of Identity!

Sigh. It's a common mistake among true believers, to assume that everyone else is incapable of thought and therefore has nothing valuable to add to the Holy Writ. Sometimes I tire of explaining that morality addresses the unique powers and dilemmas of an individual, asking 'What shall I do?' — whereas the philosophy of law fries a different kettle of fish, adjudication of disputes, custody of those who are incapable or legally forbidden to exercise their liberty, and the combined might of a community.

The purpose of law is to limit arbitrary government power and to defend innocent liberty. I admit that "innocent liberty" is a fine distinction, but fundamental fairness, trial by jury, and due process are effective tools that took centuries to discover and refine. The common law underpins everything we take for granted, including contract, property, freedom to take or quit a job, to save or spend money or give it away. This has nothing to do with legislation or a Bill of Rights. Liberty as a fully articulated legal concept predated and inspired the American Revolutionary War of Independence.

It's not so much that I want to delve into legal principles with respect to immigration and property rights. Rather, I believe we should consider how little the average person "paid" for the involuntary gift of life. No one chooses to be born, nor the time and place of his debut in a modern, prosperous industrial world not of his making. Ayn Rand suggested that 2% of us feed, clothe and shelter the other 98% by pioneering discoveries and superlative economic contributions, organizing oil production, mechanized transport, medicine and whatnot.

After touring most of the world's capitals and an infinity of rented apartments, I moved my family to a rural county in the middle of nowhere, built a nice house sheathed in steel and concrete on a tactical hill with an independent water supply. After a couple of years, I came to observe that my neighbors had certain local customs that I admired. We have a volunteer fire department, supported by semiannual picnics and bingo. Folks gather at the general store to trade gossip and plot ways to help those who were laid low by illness or injury. The next community over the ridge meets at a community center once a week to play bluegrass and share a potluck dinner. There are social networks of old "back to the land" hippies who celebrate 4th of July and Thanksgiving with happy gatherings at one of the many homesteads they developed decades ago. When we have a bad storm, everyone pitches in to clear fallen trees and put things back in order, helping those who need a hand to deal with adversity. None of it is government. They are voluntary community actions. The nearest cop is 27 miles away. Crimes and criminal conspiracy are dealt with privately in the first instance, pending review by sworn LEOs when they have time.

Nonpartisan volunteers organize the ballot box and certify the result of this tiny precinct in plebicites on funding a little school district.

Property lines are marked with fences, a few benchmarks here and there from a century ago that positively defy description — a broken axle stuck in the ground upright, a pile of rocks, a seasonal creek, a carved tree. It's not uncommon for cattle to break a fence and wander. The neighbors know who's cows belong to who. Some folks hold grudges for social slights or bad behavior that happened 20 years ago. It's not hard to make friends, but deep allegiances are family, or that rarest of species a trusted trueheart who worked for the benefit of all. I've met most of them. Wonderful people who tend cemeteries and repair churches.

To own property is nice, but roads and utility rights-of-way and neighbors make a community. Ownership in a big city is nonstop compliance with Federal, state, and local government. In a rural community like ours, none of the foregoing have an effective footprint. What happens or fails to happen is decided ad hoc by interested and active neighbors acting in concert. It is the genius of rural America that Jefferson and Franklin admired; it incubated Abe Lincoln's simple decency about ending slavery. Nowadays, it's called "flyover" country, the national breadbasket, farmers and ranchers who feed the cities, get machines and oil in trade. There are few wealthy people, many who are comfortable because they work for it constantly and rationally with taciturn pride and willingness to overcome hardships, to help one another in an emergency, of course, but likewise in routine matters like repairing a car or a tractor.

Objectivists have to get past the theoretical and live life on life's terms. The right to life is an abstract idea that has nothing to do with being born, being cared for by parents, entering into a society that intersects personhood a thousand ways — not least in the business of learning to collaborate, do the obvious, socialize, explore a world of multiple cultures and persons. I cannot for the life of me condemn someone for choosing a better life, undertaking the risk of joining a society that he/she doesn't understand immediately. It takes time to integrate. I've done it repeatedly — in Europe, in Asia and Africa, in sun-drenched Costa Rica, and now in a sparsely populated rural community in America's heartland, not unlike where I was born.

Everywhere I've traveled and learn to live with others, the rules of property meant little or nothing compared to defacto anarchy. In the most tightly regulated hellhole, liberty always trumps property. What people choose to do matters more than armed guards and walls to stop them. Normatively, they help one another, contrive ways to evade government, make friends and punish wrong-doers by boycott, escape, exercising the human right of liberty.

Let's not confuse life and liberty. If you wish to attribute all desirable qualities to an abstract ideal of "the life of a rational being" complete with dignity and liberty and property rights, it understates the life-giving aspect of Liberty — a persistent right to action, whether rational or not, dignified or absurd, rich or poor, landed or property-less. Objectivists are powerless to command others to be more rational and perfectly well behaved, which amounts to quashing their liberty, or denouncing it because their hopes and dreams might interfere with yours. A superior being of self-made soul has more freedom of action. It's not right to hammer down those who have simpler aims and less power, nor to forbid them use of their feet.

Speaking across generations

Not unnaturally I hoped to reach younger people on Facebook. I found it disheartening, no matter how carefully targeted. It's always best to assume that there's nothing wrong with anyone else, that the problem is entirely mine. I can't speak in slogans.

If I understand it correctly, young people today see no difference between Democrats and Republicans. They are deeply resentful of law enforcement and the U.S. military. Whether social justice warrior or anarchist, cat lover, fierce gun nut, or screwball mystic, the facts are uninteresting and unwanted. They feel what they feel — period.

We've been through a wave of Know Nothing madness as a society once before, in 1968, a generation of dopey hippies and street fighters who despised the Establishment. They saw themselves as stardust flower children and working class warriors, fighting for freedom and justice, without defining what those words meant. Everyone agreed that government was evil. No one saw that government was feeble and incompetent.

I was part of that cohort as a teenager, 50 years ago. We were led then (as now) by Marxists who proclaimed that government was a conspiracy of the rich to deprive as many people as possible of human rights, of equality and social justice, a fair share of the collective pie. It was horrible and chilling to hear Barack Obama use the same Marxist metaphor: "I like pie," he laughed at a rally. "Y'all like pie?"

There is no collective pie.

It's debatable whether there's any tangible wealth of any kind. If you own a home or a car, it needs maintenance. If you own a business, you're up to your ass in alligators, a constant war to keep your customers and employees happy, inventory balanced, paperwork filed. And if you think you own a piece of Amazon or Uber or Facebook? — overvalued paper, could be worthless any minute.

To my friends in law enforcement and the military, all I can do is hang my head in sympathy, offer thanks and sorrow. I know how hard it is. Benefits you were promised might not happen as advertised. All you get from civilians is a sneer — or real hell, if you have to deal with them in a crisis. I'm sorry. I wish it was otherwise.

To the rest of you, especially young knuckleheads, forget Lysander Spooner. Look around at your town, university, state government. Half of every dollar goes to "education" and health services, most of it a free ride for the worst people, young and old, who will never add a penny of value to society. Same thing at the Federal level. Two-thirds of expenditures for entitlements, growing every day, every minute. If interest rates ever climb out of zero (a policy called "financial repression") the interest on $20 trillion Federal debt will wipe out all other spending. No military, no student loans, no highways, no more payola for crooks like Elon Musk — and when it happens, our Treasury IOUs will be impossible to peddle, the price of bread and meat suddenly a problem, jobs vaporized, taxes doubled, then tripled.

Doesn't matter who you elect. Game over.

Tax evaders

Hugh Hewitt shouts it like self-evident truth, that individual rights were given by God. What the heck? Past tense, no less. Meanwhile, Dennis Prager mumbles about gradations of sin, because rabbis interpreted God's will requiring different punishments for bad behavior of various kinds, like letting your ox gore a slave, if it happens more than once or twice.

Would gentlemen be intellectually crippled and lost, if there was no Bible? One wonders if Bible study constitutes thought. But how horrible to see it as literal transciption of political dicta, complete and clear, celestial commandments from God, given thousands of years ago to nomads — translated in modern English song lyrics! — "Mine eyes have seen the glory of the coming of the Lord" to strike down enemies and reward His obedient warrior dead.

It's embarrassing. Christians and Jews ignore the Quran, calling it a fake Holy writ, ravings of an evil maniac that obligates no one. My way or the highway, huh? No surprise that peace is impossible in the Middle East, rival tribes armed to the teeth in defense of competing writs of political right, fighting over sand and water and oil to power armies of divine conquest.

What any of this malarkey has to do with the American Experiment baffles me.

Forget the slogan In God We Trust, cheap bait for school children and easily flattered mobs of voters, handing power to glib crooks. The truth is complicated. God-fearing Pilgrims were despots who bought African slaves and captured Indians to trade for more African slaves. If any of their women thought for themselves, they were accused of heresy or witchcraft and banished or put to death. Connecticut and Rhode Island exist because heretics were driven out of Massachusetts Bay Colony. Maryland was settled by Catholics, Virginia by Anglicans,

New York by secular Dutch traders who had no religion except profitable opportunity.

That's where "One Out Of Many" came from — 13 colonies with very little in common except defacto independence, separated by an ocean from the cockpit of European wars, as always an unending slaughter among True Believers with cockamamie religious writs and rival Holy empires. We played one empire against the other and hid behind trees, until it was too tiring to defeat ragtag insurgents and rumrunners backed by France and secretive Dutch lenders.

Forget the high flown God given "natural rights" of the Declaration. It was a commercial ploy to avoid taxes, kick out tax collectors. When the war ended, all 13 colonies and their Continental Congress were broke. They refused to pay Revolutionary foreign debt, Revolutionary officers or troops. General Washington did okay, however, had a fat personal expense account during the war, lived like a king, and was offered Kingship repeatedly. He didn't need it. Washington went home to his private kingdom with orchards, crops, and slaves.

The 13 new "states" couldn't agree on anything, taxed each other's commerce, and had overlapping boundaries based on Crown charters. America spiraled into debt-laden political bickering. Pretty funny that we'd revisit that stupidity in the Civil War, and again in the present!

The point, however, is zero mention of God in the U.S. Constitution. No holy writ. Jefferson prevailed in separation of church and state. Tolerance became a uniquely American idea, including tolerance and forgiveness for sloth, bad behavior, incompetence, and inclusion of every iron-fisted gang on Earth. Land of The Mosque and Home of The Undocumented.

I'll put up another post about the Federal government as it stands today, sprawling across all Seven Seas as world cop, occupying 3.4 billion square feet of offices and warehouses full of bureaucrats and unpayable IOUs. Conceived in liberty, up to our eyeballs in debt. We ought to give Donald Trump a round of applause. He drew a line in the sand, might actually rescue us from another dumpster dive into feckless Federal spending, cut Federal taxes, propound some crazy stunt like Let Freedom Ring.

Laws of nature and nature's God

It was wonderful to be born in the United States, and like most kids of my generation I said the Pledge of Allegiance in school, one Nation under God. I was compelled to attend Sunday School and catechism class in order to be confirmed in a Protestant church, more or less in the tradition of the Founding Fathers. My education pertaining to the American Revolution was idealized, a Declaration of Independence and Washington crossing the Delaware.

Later in life it became interesting and important to study everything more closely. Pilgrims purchased slaves and captured Indians to trade for more slaves. The Revolutionary War was a financial and political disaster. Everything the Founders did turned to crap, especially in the Federal Convention of 1787. Supreme Court decisions went from bad to worse, decreeing that Indians were in a permanent condition of pupilage and Negroes were inhuman. It led to Civil War with nearly a million casualties; cost five times the GNP of 1860. Worthless paper money, income tax, wars to grab territory and force trade, domestic regulation of commerce and power to compel obedience in matters of private life all flowed from the Civil War.

I made a special study of the Gilded Age. Railroads were financed with European loans and a ludicrous "curb market" for worthless securities. Conspiracies of money and corrupt politics opened the door to another bout of civil war, pitting farmers against bankers, consumers vs. producers. The Supreme Court held that the police power of Congress was an unlimited writ of arbitrary will. Regulatory agencies bloomed, liberty ring-fenced and strangled.

It's not unnatural to seek the genesis of that result. I came to see that it was one phrase in the Declaration of Independence, "the Laws of Nature and Nature's God" that entitled us to form a government of our own choosing. Quite a claim when you think about it. Signatories to the

Declaration believed themselves competent to decode God's eternal blueprint?

I made a close study of natural rights doctrine and came to despise it. Far more important to the evolution of a just society were the interests of children, our "innocent posterity" as the Declaration explained, a specific justification for war. Eventually it was expanded to include the welfare of women and children worldwide. We sent missionaries, diplomats, armies of conquest and occupation, foreign aid. At home, every state, city and village created schools to educate children and supervise their moral development. The story of Tom Sawyer and Huckleberry Finn was a saga of truancy and delinquency. In the 1930s, it was The Dead End Kids, in the 50s and 60s a wave of fashionable beatniks and smiling hippies. No matter what our government attempted to do for children, it led to woe. Today's situation is hopeless and irreversible, a nation of digital zombies and precious snowflakes crying for a "safe space" in college. Millions are employed in street crime, obscenity, socialist agitation, and fantasy roleplay, given a blank check that broke our economy and punished productive enterprise. Entertainment is not a productive industry. Neither are armies of teachers, politicians, and drill sergeants.

In reaction to the modern mess, roughly one-third of America has pledged allegiance to God again, loudly devoted to scripture, prayers, "Young Earth" geology, and the defense of Israel no matter what it costs, as if Israel was our 51st state, more important than the other fifty put together.

Our innocent progeny have never been so ill-served. Talk radio host Dennis Prager proclaims that we are in another civil war. He's an old man, a true believer in myths: E Pluribus Unum, One Nation Under God. His rear view mirror is a kinescope, gazing at Ozzie and Harriet, can't see what happened to Ricky Nelson, one of the disgusting delinquents who dishonored his parents and the Obedient Generation of television households, advertisers, NFL football, and Thanksgiving dinners. Today, Prager announced happily that Trump is "a conservative dream" — which is true, but not in the sense that Prager meant. Donald Trump is a TV personality, no different than Barack Obama.

Trump's presidency is toast because he's not Obama.

It's folly to bemoan ignorance of or indifference to Natural Law and God-given Rights. They have no weight in legislation, merely an empty gesture in the Constitution that prohibits religious tests to hold public office, which is universally honored in the breach. No politician dares to admit that he's an atheist or freethinker. Paul Ryan was compelled to disavow Ayn Rand.

Worse — power politics rule the world, and we're outnumbered by those who have no Judeo Christian God to complicate their aspirations. The only way to prevail would be nuclear war, incinerating their innocent progeny and our own, a final and irreversible farewell salute to Nature.

What's wrong with the world?

Some of my friends are upset that Donald Trump is president. Others are alarmed about the possibility of war with North Korea. Microsoft is mad that NSA hacking tools were stolen (?) and used to launch a global ransomware attack that clobbered Europe and Asia. Fifteen hours a day, conservative talk radio worries about Israel. Black Americans are angry about policing. White Americans are horrified by crime. European bureaucrats are demanding tens of billions from Britain to fund EU pensions as a price of exiting the EU. American college students won't tolerate "hate speech" on campus, and they're agitating for free education and health care. U.S. doctors are quitting the profession in droves, and health insurers are withdrawing from state after state, losing money. Republicans can't seem to pass new legislation of any kind, despite holding a majority in both houses of Congress, with a Republican White House. The geniuses at Google want gender equality in entertainment, more screen time for women. Russia worries about bellicose American posturing, and we condemn Russia for a long list of wrongs. Meanwhile, China, Japan, and Saudi Arabia are bankrupt, skating on thin ice papered over with debt. Another Wall Street crash is inevitable, merely a question of when.

All of these concerns and conflicting interests are, uh, fine.

What's wrong with the world, in my view, is something slightly different. People have lost sight of how recently we became well-fed and prosperous, blithely unconscious of liquid energy production. At the moment, oil is cheap because we're using less, but oil supplies are flowing from rusting rigs in the Gulf of Mexico through a crumbling infrastructure of pipelines built 50+ years ago. Shale has never made a dime of "full cycle" net profit, except wet gas production in the Marcellus, cheap fuel for heating and cooling New York, Boston, Phila-delphia, Baltimore, and Washington DC, served by new pipelines and newly built gas-fired power plants, but that has nothing to do with crude oil or refined products like gasoline, diesel, and jet fuel, liquid energy for food production and transport.

Oil matters first, most, and always because it powers 95% of U.S. transportation. Farm to market. Bunker fuel for ships. Passenger cars. Jet aircraft. Heavy equipment for construction and mining. Asphalt for roads. Lubricants that every machine, every pump, everything with wheels has to have, including our commercial fleet of 350,000 big rigs and 25,000 diesel rail locomotives. Oil is our industrial lifeblood. No oil means no food or water or machines or plastics.

Hate plastic, do you? Without plastic there's no sterile surgery, no medical labs, no packaging, no consumer products like bleach, cell phones, cosmetics, bottled soda and chips. You need oil, every day all day and night to survive, because you and your family are absolutely unfit to live like cavemen or nomads, subsisting hand-to-mouth on roots and berries and wild game.

Sorry, electric cars and solar panels are expensive toys, less than 2% of the energy picture, if you include wind farms, biomass, gas-powered buses and vans. Tesla could not exist without lavish Federal and California subsidies, borrowed government cash at work for the unearned benefit of "ecologically minded" oil consumers. No oil? — no food in grocery stores, no tractors or harvesters, no meat, milk, cheese, wheat, sugar, orange juice, or pots and pans.

Living without oil is not a good option, however much you want to "save the planet." People are eager to live better and healthier, not worse and sickly and poor. If you have a job, it's because oil powers it. If you need a cop or an ambulance, they operate on oil. Electrical wire insulation and plumbing parts are made from oil. Global trade runs on oil. Without imports and exports, your cost of living would skyrocket. WalMart and Apple would shut their doors, unable to perform the miracle of sourcing products from China, Korea, Thailand, Malaysia.

It's pretty simple, really. No oil? — no carpeting or vinyl under your feet, no roof over your head, no furniture or furnace. And I certify that crude is not an inexhaustible resource. Most of it is in Russia and the Middle East, a few puddles in war-torn, corrupt Africa.

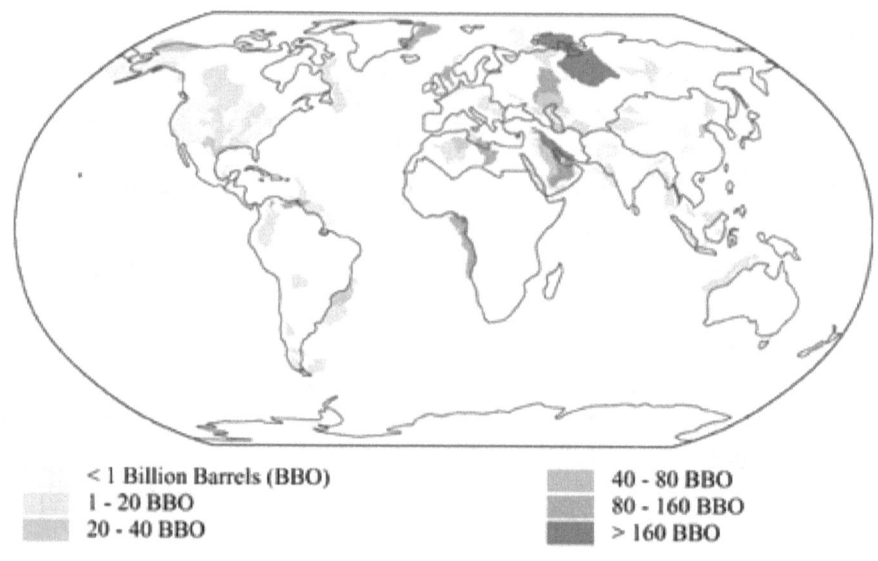

< 1 Billion Barrels (BBO)

1 - 20 BBO

20 - 40 BBO

40 - 80 BBO

80 - 160 BBO

> 160 BBO

Two world wars, 1914-18 and 1939-45, were fought over crude. Germany had no oil. Britain had no oil. Japan had no oil. They fought over oil wells in Romania, Persia, and the Dutch East Indies. America prevailed because we were the world's #1 oil producer at the time. We built planes and ships by the tens of thousands, transported millions of soldiers and supplied them with food and fuel and weapons that no one else on earth could hope to match, because we were rich with oil. But by 2003, we were reduced to seizing Iraqi oil (temporarily), a plan that failed because Americans did not grok what was happening or why. Wars are fought for oil, not "nation building" or purple ink on somebody's finger.

When you consider that most of the remaining oil is in Russia and Arabia, our foreign policy becomes a lot less confusing. Strip out the noise and bluster about human rights. We want to stay on cordial terms with oil producers, because world peace and prosperity depends on the oil trade. Freedom of the seas means supertanker oil exports to Japan, Germany, China, and (yep) the United States. Britain will join the list soon, because North Sea wells have declined in production, after 50 years of heroically exploiting it to the last drop of oil.

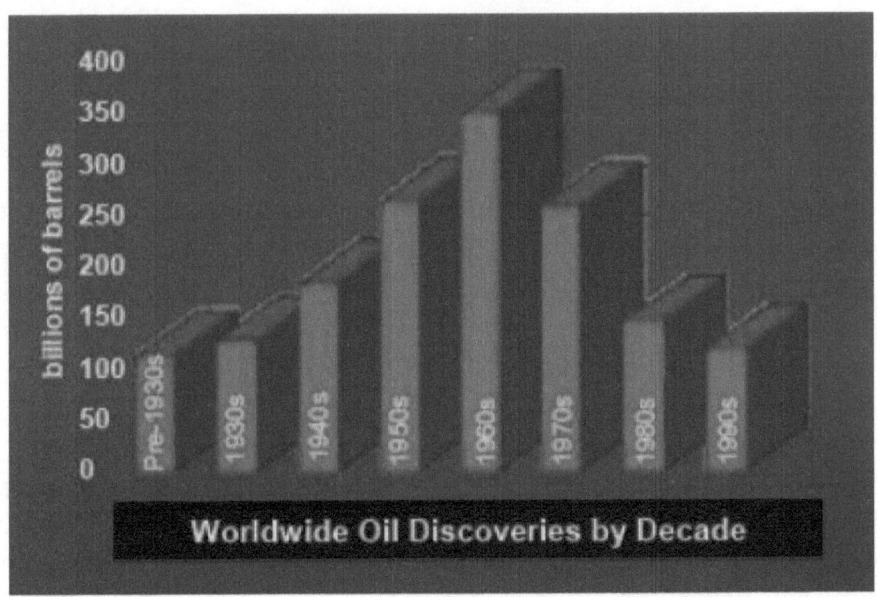

It is an uncomfortable fact of science that oil exists because organic matter and carbonates were buried by millions of years of erosion and sand and silt. No dinosaurs involved, none. Geologists and drillers became good at finding oil in saturated rock worldwide. What they found also was pretty scary, that the "elephants" (huge oil resources) were few and known, no happy surprises left anywhere on Earth. What we've been doing in the 21st century is to scrape the bottom of the barrel, expensive fracking, tar sands, little discoveries in ultradeep water or international joint ventures with crooks in Kazakhstan and Siberia.

At the moment, you can't feel it, because the U.S. economy is stagnant, no growth, and low demand for oil has held the price down. Worldwide oil production is sufficient to limp along comfortably at present with a hidden cost. It's hollowing out Saudi Arabia's finances and shut down unprofitable Canadian and U.S. production. Not good news. We're in an "energy trap" economically.

If demand picks up, the price of oil will rise and stunt growth. If there's a recession like 2009 again, oil companies will go bankrupt or consolidate and shed staff. Oil exploration is not a wildly profitable business, despite folklore about pioneer wildcatters and Gilded Age oil barons. To fear and resent today's oil companies, like they were 19th century "robber barons" is more than stupid. It's willful disregard for factual data, clinging to an old conspiracy theory that expired long before you and I were born. All oil companies in the United States are competitive, publically traded companies, struggling to eke out a profit on declining wells and rising costs. Many are losing money.

Most people think Big Oil is a safe investment and they buy shares of Exxon, Chevron, Shell for pension funds and retirement portfolios. Dividends are paid every quarter. But there's no astronomical triple-digit growth like Apple, Amazon, or Google.

Oil is more high tech than most of the tech giants in Silicon Valley. Take my word for it as an insider oil industry analyst. We use more computing power to search for, develop, and produce oil than any other private or public activity, including military forces. The F-35 is a marvelous new aircraft with high tech controls — a drop in the bucket compared to oil company supercomputers and the capital investment required for a single new deepwater installation.

It might help a little to lighten up various Executive Orders and regulatory hurdles that block offshore exploration in California — but, really, it doesn't matter at this point. Our problems are much bigger than that, specifically pipeline infrastructure. Keystone XL does not fix it. There are tens of thousands of miles of pipelines in North America that are nearing or already past the end of their service life, slowly being eaten by corrosion. If bridges need maintenance, imagine what iron pipe buried underground or in saltwater looks like.

I wish it were that simple, print a trillion dollars of public money to replace our pipelines and refurbish refineries — but it's not worth it. Soon there will be less and less oil to pump through existing infrastructure and deliver to your neighborhood gas station by tank truck.

When crude oil went to $100 a barrel, it hammered demand. We drove fewer miles and did without expensive meat and fish, bought fewer cars, shopped for bargains. Oil fell sharply, then crashed again, struggled for equilibrium in the New Normal of economic stagnation. North Dakota is kaput at $50 a barrel, and storage at Cushing is full.

That's the good news. We can fill up our cars $2 a gallon unleaded in the Midwest, always more expensive in California because they have higher taxes and transport costs. It doesn't matter what the price of gasoline is today.

The problem is a darker future when U.S. firms produce less oil.

The remaining oil reserves in North America are difficult to find and expensive to drill. Most of the world's oil reserves are Russian. Forget the stupid Saudis and Venezuela in the grip of civil war, twin disasters that cannot be remedied, not even by force of arms. Ditto Iran and Iraq, mired in prayer and endemic graft. And Africa is worse.

It's conceivable that the U.S. could work with Russia, but we have to rethink our diplomatic strategy, stop talking about Putin like he's an evil monster. Rapprochement will not be easy. Not that long ago Exxon, BP, and Shell got shafted in joint ventures with Russian partners.

It's good that Rex Tillerson was nominated and confirmed as Secretary of State. The Exxon CEO knows as well as anyone does how important it is to develop new joint venture projects. The press had palpitations when President Trump met with Russian officials at the White House, but that's what a working relationship will require, open handed diplomacy and cooperation.

Alternatively, we could invade and conquer Mexico, fire everyone at Pemex and auction off vast ultradeep blocks in the Gulf — but I don't think anyone has enough money to gamble on the Perdido Fold Belt, complicated geology far from the existing pipeline network.

That's the problem in deepwater Brazil, too, uneconomic tight oil under three miles of water plus two miles of gooey salt under a rugged seafloor that precludes pipelaying. It doesn't matter what the Brazilian politicians and brainless bureaucrats think they're doing with structured finance, cushy union jobs for ill-trained hardhats, and Chinese loans. It's uneconomic tight oil.

I want to end on a positive note. But that would be lying.

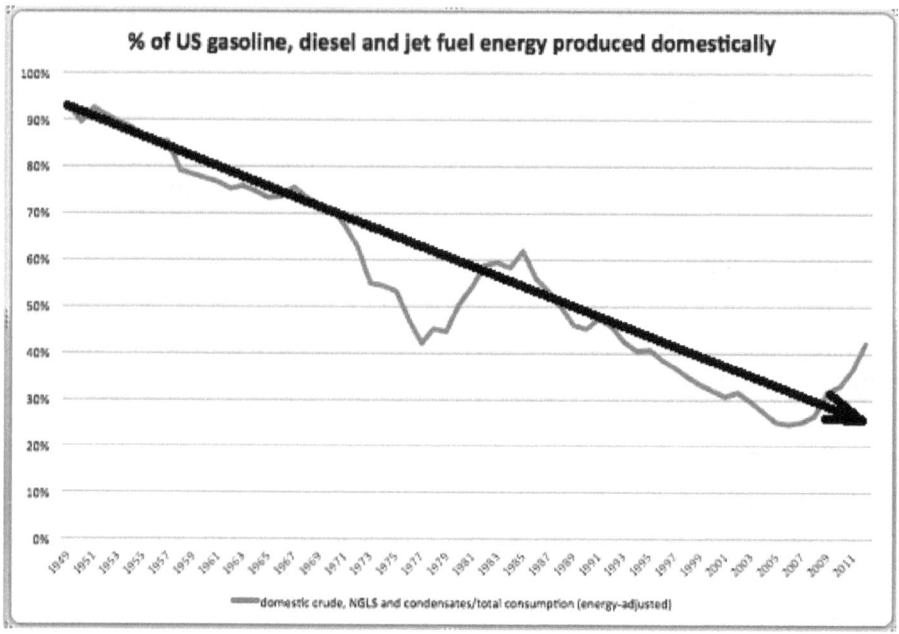

% of US gasoline, diesel and jet fuel energy produced domestically

domestic crude, NGLS and condensates/total consumption (energy-adjusted)

U.S. crude oil production is in long-term decline. There was a little boost from Prudhoe in Alaska and another boost from the Bakken and Eagle Ford shale, but they were blips compared to growing demand for oil since World War II. America is destined to be a net importer forever, to sustain what we've become, a pampered society that drives cars and flies commercial jets and eats well because farms are mechanized and food is trucked to cities and surburbs.

What ordinary people can do about this problem is "reduce, reuse, recycle." Our future will be less dependent on transport. It's always good to spend less and save more for a rainy day — in this case, a rainy day with no car in the driveway, crowded buses, and fewer selections available at Kroger and Whole Foods. I know that sounds dire, horrible gloom and doom.

Fixing it is a question of working with the Russians. It's time to end the Cold War. Our future prosperity does not require defense of Israel or Saudi Arabia or Iraq. It requires a partnership with Russia, strategically and industrially. If we refuse, the Chinese will eat our lunch.

About directing

Dave Pauwels was kind enough to ask about my experiences as a director. I don't see much difference between film and tape, analog or digital, drama, comedy, or documentary, so I'll talk about them generally as "filmed entertainment" — a traditional term that distinguishes movies from theater. I did some theatrical coaching for a community production, because lovely Beth had the lead role as Anna in The King and I, and she needed help, but I never directed "legitimate theater" and never wanted to. It was visually boring and empty.

Screen format matters, so a film director thinks in terms of Academy 1.33, letterbox 1.85, old fashioned 4:3 TV, and modern 16x9. A very long time ago, Fred Waller talked about a "dynamic frame" for his Cinerama format, and I have pals who worked on IMAX pix. I made 3-D product, side-by-side, over-under, anaglyph (colored glasses), silvered screen (polarized glasses) and "autosteroscopic" (no glasses). I worked in Super 8mm, 16mm, Super 16mm, 35mm, 1/2" VHS, 3/4" U-Matic, Hi-8, 1" B format, 1" C format, BetaSP, 4:2:2, DV, HD, and 4K.

Cameras are funny things. I've used tiny ones strapped to my head for "subjective camera" scenes, medium size for Steadicam and Flight Stick moving shots, heavy Eclair NPR handheld for drama, and massive Ikegami 99A camcorders for news packages, all sorts of dollies and booms, high platforms, fork lifts, cherry pickers, wheelchair, and utility crane.

My first 16mm camera was a Cine Special that took 50-ft magazines that had to be loaded in total darkness. Then an Auricon with 200-ft loads, after which I stopped buying cameras. I learned to rent equipment according to what the project required and fell in love with Arriflex and Aaton. I also stopped doing camera work in 1973, hired camera operators and professional DPs who were better than I was, although I continued to express opinions about lighting.

There is a great deal of specialization in filmed entertainment, most significant of which are the Department Heads. I've worked with brilliant art directors, choreographers, prop masters and designers, animators, sound engineers, musicians, vocalists, film editors and modern Final Cut mavens. It's not necessary for a director to know technical trades. The job of directing is to make the movie, not to operate the equipment. There are a lot of folks who make movies without division of labor, shooting and editing all by themselves. I didn't like it. One cannot direct the cast and envision the scene while futzing with exposure and sound equipment.

The serious business of editing is not something that I entrust blindly to an editor, however talented he/she might be with keyboard commands and data files. In television production, it's a little different because the schedule is so compressed. A great editor matters. However, I always directed the edit of certain sequences, especially musical performances with a lot of coverage, usually 3 "iso" cameras x 2 takes = 6 angles, one master shot, the rest in tight close-ups and a couple moving shots. Use of screen time and montage, how pictures join and move the eye, are signature aspects of filmmaking. We're constrained by takes that are marked as "Print" and the awkward lapses of continuity in other takes. It's hell trying to piece together verité (spontaneous coverage of a one-time event, no other footage). Compromises are a delicate job. Directors make silk purses from all sorts of junk.

True likewise in directing performers.

Supporting cast is a recurring problem. They only have a few lines, and they're often frightened when suddenly they're facing a big crew, hot lights, and have to do close-ups. I let them try, then we try something else, spend a little extra time with them. In all projects large and small the pressure of money is constant, so it mustn't be wasted, but a bad performance won't do. Directors balance on a high-wire with one eye on the clock and the other on quality.

This is especially true of "indie" directors who work with tight budgets, but true also of A-list pix. The budget is a budget whatever size. You have a certain number of shooting days and travel days, very tightly constrained and busy pre-production and post.

THE PROJECT

Sigh. Directors spend 7/8 of their time doing things other than directing. At the beginning of every project, there is a concept or property (book, screenplay, scenario, live event). Money must be discussed with producers, stars, agents, investors, and distribution toads, all of whom have inappropriate suggestions that have to be politely turned aside. Crews make suggestions. Directing is diplomacy from first day to last in pre-production, on the set, and in post. Worst of all is "talking a good show" in someone's office or a restaurant.

Whether directors should write their own material is a thrawn conundrum. I believe that the profession of original screenwriting is a high art in its own right, and I know for a fact that my much beloved writer friends have far better ideas than I do. Erik Svehaug wrote a short story that blew my mind, screaming to be filmed as written, although it needs screen adaptation. Rob Williamson, Hal Badt, Joey Neniu, Lola Teigland, Rene Barnes, Dave Pauwels, and Naomi Distill wrote scripts that I very much admired and wished I could film.

However (big sigh) there is no screenplay that should be shot as written, in my experience. A director is a villain to many talented artists. We change things that they crafted with love and care and skillfulness. True also of directing the cast and crew, especially stars. Directors direct them, treat them as living clay to be lifted, smashed as gently and firmly as possible, always in their corner, always grateful for their willingness to listen. Same thing with screenwriters. Love 'em to bits, appreciative of genius, delighted by surprising material I could not have created. Sorry, I want to change this this this this this this and this. Need a second draft and script doctors, scene cards (argh!) and my hand on the final script. This is not good news. A director will put his signature style on the script, which producers and stars dislike. Money talks, and directors do not have the same weight as a bankable A-list movie star.

That's why I liked working with small stars and semi-pro talent.

One less obstacle to fight. Producers are bad enough, and agents of all stripes are demons from hell, determined to destroy whoever they touch or refuse to touch with a twelve-foot Polecat (an expandable ceiling speader used in lighting an interior).

THE PRODUCTION

Whatever the project may be, long or short, big budget or nearly none, one begins with the leitmotif, an era in time, a look, a feeling that will inhabit the project and determine how it's played, photographed, designed and costumed, edited and mixed — always with an audience and release format in mind.

The director is a Temporary Audience more than a chief artist, although he has to be chief artist as well, plus crew chief, front office knight errant, and on occasion Liar-In-Chief when someone throws a hissy fit about a saxophone being damaged by a gaffer pulling power cables across the set. Yes, absolutely, we'll pay for it I lied to get the damn 15-piece Afro Cuban Jazz horn section miked up for a quick rehearsal and complicated camera coverage on a flashy disco floor with dancers in costume.

I always went for elegant and intelligent as a signature style. Some projects were modern, others in a futuristic fantasy setting, or time-less, or a historical period. How well this can be executed depends heavily on the skill and energy of a production designer, working to an artistic vision that the director has to communicate to everyone in front of and behind the camera.

Production sound aims at clarity, although it's understood we will "loop" most of the dialogue in post on a big show. Little shows live or die on sound quality recorded on set or sometimes in adverse exterior set-ups with traffic noise.

Set-ups are a specific camera position, shooting film style. When I was a youngster, I tried to work 2-camera and gave it up pretty quickly. So, each set-up implies a lighting set-up that has to make sense when we do a reverse angle later.

Backgrounds are a bitch to control, if you're working in a "practical" interior like a hotel room, conference room, storefront, etc. Windows have to be scrimmed with black nets to cut intense sunlight, key light balanced for daylight color temperature. Big pain in the ass for 20 seconds of screen time. That's why I care deeply about hardworking gaffers and grips. I ask for the moon and hurry up, please — but I also make compromises they know nothing about, because my directions are always mindful of crew capabilities, available stands, soft goods, expendables, and how long I dare to delay start of shoot. A big crew and vast resources are a different kind of problem. Set-ups still matter, and they have to be communicated through chains of command.

Funny way to talk about directing, that it amounts to a military command. Sorry. That's largely true. When to start and stop, what to do next, sudden improvisation, unscheduled retakes, and a million decisions affecting every department are the business of directing. It's tiring to direct 12 hours a day, and it is emphatically lonely work. As you can imagine, I made a lot of mistakes as a young director, and none was as bad as sitting down at a crew lunch table. All conversation stopped. You can't chum around and smile if you're the director. Everyone on the set, both cast and crew, are attentive to and endlessly puzzled by the director's enigmatic personality. He must NOT need approval. It's fatal to morale, snaps the spell of confidence in his leadership, and the director MUST lead at all times.

Cast and crew come and go, some only working for a few days, others a few weeks, but the director starts and finishes the entire project. He must be at home in recording studios, edit suites, legal conferences, casting, food fights with the screenwriter, etc. I was always very appreciative of intelligent, well-organized producers, production managers, unit managers, and assistant directors — all of whom are functionaries who control resources without influencing the creative work, except in limiting what's possible by budget constraints that translate into shooting days.

The deep truth of filmmaking is awful. We shoot out-of-sequence. That means each scene must be alive in the here and now PLUS make sense when it's joined to something shot on another day or another week, miles from whatever's happening now on the set. That's why the front office people matter. They have to provide everything out-of-sequence, the right cast, crew, props, costumes, picture cars, on the day and hour when it's needed. Huge enterprise on a feature film. Not exactly trivial on smaller projects, either, considering that production staff is proportionately smaller. In corporate work, the "producer" is a writer-director with a skeleton crew of two, cameraman and a utility gaffer/boom operator. Barrel of fun.

On the set of a larger show for cinemas or TV, the director has a small group to support him. The script supervisor marks each set-up and each take on her copy of the script in a binder, noting how long each take ran, how far down the page, and a zillion continuity notes. Who picked up the banana, in which hand, on which line, and how it was peeled, how far, when. Multiply that by every player, every angle, every moving camera shot. The assistant director is likewise at the director's side the instant his director walks on the set, which he announces with a loud voice and electric bell: "Director on the set!" — which means to seek permission to carry on doing whatever the crew was doing, or be ready to undo something. The 1st A.D. also has responsibility for the principal cast. It's never predictable that actors will show up unless a car is sent for them and other arrangements made to pry them off the ceiling, feed and water everyone, get them into costume and make-up on time. Jeez. Couldn't do that job if my life depended on it, and a good 1st A.D. is worth his weight in platinum. Big shows supply a director's chair, emergency food and drink on set, and an intelligent production assistant whose job it is to be a personal "dogsbody" for the screwball director going through hell.

Why it always has to be hell, I don't know. Broadly speaking, you only get one chance to get it right. Whatever happens in front of and behind the camera must be done efficiently, easily, naturally, with as little hesitation as possible. The schedule is crushing. Today we must make 3 pages. Tomorrow we must make 4 pages. Jesus F. Christ!

Above it all is the final movie, whether made of a million pieces shot out-of-sequence or only a couple hundred. The assembled puzzle must make seamless entertainment with originality and verve. Stunts have to be convincing, the extras and picture cars have to move at an exact moment, and each performance — the smallest expression of reaction — must be authentic, thrilling or hilarious, as the case may be, despite the fact that successive takes often get worse, not better. I limited myself to 5 takes. I never had the luxury of endless time and money, nor is that the primary reason to get a great performance in a few takes, with at least one extra take for "protection." Performers wear out fast, get stuck in a rut, lose the excitement of filming a new scene. Directors have to ignite them during a quick walk-through to rehearse follow focus, pan and tilt, moving shot on track, or whatever the set-up happens to be. With cast energized and props in place, the magic word "Action" must not be diluted with fatigue or uncertainty or tedium. Same thing with the crew. They work their asses off and must have relaxation when a good take is marked "Print!"

Directing is the art of creative leadership, constantly envisioning the whole movie that will someday be edited and mixed. On small projects, everything runs like lightning, has to be done extremely well, quickly. The chief problem on shows of all sizes is human limitation. Everyone on the set including the director can get it 80% okay, never 100% correct. That's why we say: "When the shooting stops, the filmmaking begins."

WORKING WITH ACTORS AND FAMOUS PEOPLE

If the show is properly staffed, with highly competent people in every department, the job of directing narrows and focusses on staging and eliciting the work of performers in front of the camera, whether scripted or impromptu. The director has to spread a certain kind of creative soil, a calm happy place, smoothing over brief delays for technical reasons. He must be alive to the inner soul of actors and famous people, all of whom are naturally pissed off, surly, and doubtful that this will be good for their careers. They come to the set with sidekicks, agents, children, stomach aches, sneezes, and hung over. No one is convinced that they will be paid as agreed, and it is CERTAINLY not enough money to justify what is requested.

That's why middle men and PR people matter. Show business is entirely a question of Who's Who and Who Knows Who. I was doing a fairly good job of managing a three-ring circus of scheduled musical acts and a dozen celebrity interviews three camera "iso" for intimate coverage, hoping to get a few good minutes from each 20-minute chat — when Matt Freud walked in with Chrissie Hynde. This is why directors have headsets. I scrambled my best interviewer, two cameras, a sound man, and a handheld "basher" with spun diffusion to get set up in a blink. I mean a fucking BLINK, as fast as they could run and roll to record before Chrissie got bored and decided to do something else, like leave the nightclub. She was wonderful. Best clip in the show. My job was talk to her and beam casual good vibes, as an equal, until the crew was in place and rolling. I had to make it fun for her, introduce her to the gal who was going to interview her. Then step back and let it happen without interfering. Directors only get one shot at doing the right thing.

Filmed drama or scripted comedy is a completely different kettle of fish, but it remains very much a question of Who's Who and Who Knows Who, whether on an A-list feature or a zero budget indie project. I'll talk about each in turn, starting with w.k. (well known) star talent. Directing is diplomacy in casting, a moment of magic in a chance encounter. Stars are people who've seen it all, especially oodles of hollowness and glassy-eyed fans. The director has to be someone they immediately like and want to talk to further, career commitments and big enough money permitting. It is never easy, unless a director has real chops as a human being. I don't know why I was drawn to it, but I started working with all kinds of people as a teenage filmmaker — girls, boys, Hell's Angels, cameramen, dangerous stunt action, university actors, crazy musicians, recording studio engineers. By the time I had ten or twelve projects under my belt, I got assignments in Australia and Holland, my first brush with pro crews and a few famous people.

At this juncture I should recite the advice I gave in an article on Psychology of Free Expression, viz: "Hold your own with the men, and make love to the women."

Both are useful for a beginner, but directing is something additional and less simple. The job becomes a vessel of enjoyment for all concerned. It's done respectfully, at arm's length until we're on the set, deal negotiated and signed, with hot lights and a big crew on deck, waiting patiently. Then it's an intimate romance that's confined to private eyes that no one else can see, words whispered very close that no one else can hear — although at times, it's good to goof a little and smile out loud, express honest satisfaction that everyone on set can see and hear after a good take. I've cried on the set, laughed, shouted, frowned. But the relationship with star talent must be personal and private, deeply rooted in trust.

This is equally true of low budget projects with amatuer and semi-pro talent. They come with enthusiasm and delusions, tire easily if something is badly organized, need to be understood and helped as people who want to go forward somehow in show business. Small shows are done painfully fast, with difficult set-ups. Directing is always diplomacy and love making at arm's length, until we have hot camera and I need to smile and say "Action!" It does not work unless the talent knows what I want from them. We do a few takes and suddenly it's easy.

That's because famous stars and total Unknowns are alike in many ways. They need to see it's possible to be involved with an exciting project, something worth doing because the director knows his stuff. Okay, we fight about story and money. Okay, we compromise. They're always shocked when I say it's the actor's job to decide what the scene is about, how to play it. Not just a formality or covert diplomacy. I mean it. I can help shape whatever they see in the script, but the performance comes from the performer, and it's always good to plant that seed early in a relationship. On the set, they come with big stuff that needs to be trimmed, or nervous and lost. Directors know what to do with raw, slightly wobbly material, thinking of how it will play in close-up, reverses, and how it must join to the next shot, the next scene with other actors and parallel action.

No one does this perfectly. Directors are perhaps the least able people on earth, the most vulnerable at times, easily overwhelmed and overthrown, outnumbered by cast and crew and frustrated production staff. So, the job of directing is ESSENTIALLY to direct oneself, budget one's creativity and confident diplomacy. Whenever possible, the director must leave the set, detach from all responsibility, talk to no one, lay down and rest, eat and drink privately. He will be summoned soon enough when the next set-up is ready.

I lived all my life to do this work. I made a few rules along the way. Never watch TV shows or movies made by others. Treat oneself to nice restaurants. Wear nice clothing and comfortable shoes, change socks two or three times each day in production. Don't worry, but check the dailies. I seldom look through the lens. I know the focal length and know what it sees without looking. No zooms. No handheld unless it's a POV shot. Framing matters and must be communicated extremely clearly. Take what you get, try not to worry, and fix it in post.

A destination

Dennis Prager is a damn fool, but occasionally he says something provocative. Today, he said normal people have a detailed map of every street, but no idea where they want to go, a destination. Forget that destination is a bad bluff that implies Destiny, which is Prager's stock in trade, with Ten Commandments, sin, hell, and equally stupid notions about Israel.

So, let's call it choice of adventure, going somewhere new. Wonderful to consider what an anarcho-capitalist free society would be like.

Surprise! — it's not much different than personal life today. You can join a tribe or remain independent, raise a family or remain aloof and alone, uncomplicated. There's no cop to direct the traffic of your Ambition, another interesting word that implies the reach of one's arm, an ambit. In a fully free society, you and I are limited by the size and shape of physical body in the fullest sense, because your mind is part of your physical body. We grow from a little stone of DNA to the primitive animality of childhood and an unfolding adult potential, paradoxically by folding and convoluting, growing mentally compli-cated by knowledge and experience, most of it by choice, especially the hard choice of physical courage.

I wish I was more courageous, as well as taller and smarter.

My colleague Billy Beck asked an interesting question yesterday (note in passing that Billy is infinitely more complicated than Dennis Prager, also more physically courageous than I am, a double whammy of earned, richly deserved distinction). Billy asked where the hell the idea of "nonprofit organizations" came from. I replied that it was Ben Franklin's idea, simple stuff like fire brigades and libraries. That's not entirely true, of course, because volunteer groups had a long history in Nonconformist churches, Quakers and whatnot, a Committee of Safety in Boston that launched the American Revolutionary War. Civilization needs nonprofit public associations like schools, libraries, universities, border and immigration control, Coast Guard, harbor masters, and national defense. We live in the physical world and need to address the notion of territorial boundaries. It doesn't matter how big the territory might be. Alaska has an excellent chance of becoming an independent nation, easily defined and defended, but the defense of Alaska will have to be implemented by a voluntary nonprofit organization no different than a state that no one owns and will never be profitable.

If you're familiar with The Freeman's Constitution, you know it prohibits taxation. That's why I said repeatedly in subsequent work that an Executive and a participatory legislative body to control it was needed. The best solution is a private consortium of banks, insurance companies, and wealthy "new money" entrepreneurs. Let them bid for a vote to control the state, a unique public corporation, preferred shares that will change hands from time to time. Better than democracy. We've had plenty of experience with universal suffrage, sufficient to say to hell with it. Nothing but economic and social pain when you poll easily-led nitwits who vote for public largesse and foreign wars of choice that make us less safe, less prosperous, and less free of state regulation. A privately-held "government" forbidden to levy taxes, directed by conservative large scale enterprises like banks and insurers will provide skimpy but adequate national defense, because they have skin in the game, a lot to lose. Not coincidentally, this is how the American Revolutionary War was funded. It pays to read U.S. history. Businessmen like Robert Morris and John Hancock ponied up big sums of hard money.

Flash forward to 1988 and a much smaller problem, a forest fire in rural Cazadero. I was one of a dozen neighbors who responded to fight the blaze with hand tools, because it threatened our homes, until a helicopter doused us with fire retardant and gave us a chance to win. That helicopter could have been a voluntarily subscribed service, no different than a co-op electric utility. But there's more to the story. One of our wealthier neighbors obtained an old used fire engine (yay!) that needed a garage to store it. We chipped in for lumber and spent two days hammering and sawing — a volunteer barn raising, no different than legacy 19th century American Experience when neighbors helped one another without thinking twice about it. They fought hostile Indians and rode together as a posse to catch bandits. The rule of law was observed whenever possible, another voluntary nonprofit idea led by lawmen and lawyers. Good to read U.S. history. Lawyers like Madison and Hamilton gave us the U.S. Constitution, our legacy of fair trial by jury, adversarial due process, presumption of innocence.

Obviously, the U.S. Constitution failed spectacularly, resulted in the Civil War and its idiotic aftermath, one man one vote populism, paper money, etc — but common law persisted and kept the growth of Federal government from becoming a totalitarian tyranny until very recently.

I acknowledge we're in a tough jam now, NSA monitoring every citizen, hopelessly bankrupt as a nation, zero possibility of cutting the size and scope of Federal, state, regional, or local governments. There are 85,000 branches of administrative tyranny in every corner of national life, from school districts to nuclear submarines on patrol worldwide, subsidies and payola that distort every farm, factory, hospital, highway, and household. Getting rid of government is not going to be an easy or comfortable task. Even talking about change upsets people.

We're in for a rocky ride as things fall apart. Best to prepare, of course.

One of the best ways to prepare is to form nonprofit volunteer community groups of sensible neighbors — doctors, lawyers, local bankers, businesses — not to vote for anything, but to talk about a future with less effective government, when things fall apart at an increasing pace of panic and public confusion. Think local. Be frank and share knowledge, talk about providing things your community will need and want, especially a library of libertarian history that stretches from Magna Carta to The Freeman's Constitution, centuries of common sense and courage to inspire a new kind of frontier society. Another library: practical knowledge of how to feed ourselves, produce energy, build machines, provide medical care. Technologies that a Politically Correct county librarian neglected to shelve in adequate detail and depth.

Our destination isn't destiny — it's hard choices in the face of peril, something beyond what one man or woman might do as an individual. Strong communities matter.

An idle Saturday

It's miserable being idle, completely unnatural to me. Oh, sure, there's the never ending business of publicity — but being on strike as an author is a drag. I'm ill-suited to it.

There are little chores like weed whacking, an hour to beat back insistent Nature, carve a wide swath to the barn and the pump house across the road where I store my daughter's bicycle. Last month I spent two days weed whacking to flatten several acres. I deemed it was important as a statement of occupancy, announcing to the world that I was still here and my property was guarded and cared for — and also a practical measure to fight off copperheads, at least to have a better chance of seeing them. "Snakes in the grass" became a meaningful concept when I moved here several years ago. The Ozarks are full of deadly hazards.

In the winter I have little chores, haul firewood from the barn to the house, chop soft pine lumber scrap for kindling, although I have no expectation of doing it next winter. I have $600 in cash, not enough to make it through summer, no prospect of earning another penny. As a practical matter, I gave up the notion of employment, driving 50 miles a day to a minimum wage job, if such a job existed and they overlooked my personality, an intellectual city boy in simple, unsmiling God's Country. A great place to retire. Terrible place to earn a living.

Three years ago — or was it four? — I worked a few months in Houston, suit and tie and clean shaven, star marketing writer on the 10th floor, hobnobbing with Eagle Scout executives and particularly dense marketing people in the oil patch. There was an overweight fellow who'd stop by my cubicle and suggest we go outside together for a smoke break. Poor sap couldn't write, banged together whatever his boss dictated and then came to me for editing help. I remember telling him one day at the smokers table that however long I was employed on the 10th floor, it would be the last job I'd have. True enough. Too old and ugly now. Incapable of smiling like a three dollar bill, feigning enthusiasm for outrageous lies and half-truths.

Now don't get the wrong idea. I'm perfectly capable of telling lies and half-truths for publicity purposes. I stopped doing it for other people, that's all. When I fib about my books, widows and orphans won't suffer. I know it for a fact because I have no investors, no fiduciary duty of due diligence and transparency. I'm too small for public office and disqualified as an ex-felon, so there is no urgent imperative to join a church and pretend to worry about Israel.

It is now 11:30 a.m. I need to fill six hours, somehow, before I trundle back up the hill and sit in a closet with a mattress on the floor and a wifi connection, to post this note and see what other people are talking about on Facebook, my latest "cunning plan" to win notoriety. Hah. Baldrick strikes again. Goodreads was a bust. LinkedIn.com is a wasteland as far as I can tell. My Blogger posts attract no readers and no comments. Care too much for my life and my loved ones to do something crazy. Darn it.

Twice on previous Saturdays I was occupied by radio interviews, three hours on air in frozen Fairbanks, guest of a wonderful host who's twice my size, runs a difficult business that employs 25 men, and has eight children to support. Truly admirable man. Everything I'm not.

Maybe I'll stroll half a mile to my neighbor's homestead, borrow a plug of pot, get stoned. It always helps to pass the time — except that it causes me to envision new adventures of love and life-giving courage. I don't want to reread my work again, however wonderful. I know every word of every book by heart.

I hate being idle, unwanted and unread, on strike.

Anthony Patch

I'll begin with an aside, a detour. There are three typos in my latest, not too shabby in over 103,000 words, about the same rate of goofs as Atlas Shrugged in Signet paperback 50 years ago. I wrote to Kalberman and stuck my tongue out, promptly blackballed for it.

As much as I enjoy tall tales, I wasn't inspired by Rand or RLS. Who's inspired by hamburger and pickles? The author of first rank in my heart without second or third was Scott Fitzgerald, which should not require explanation. But since you haven't read him, I'll idle a while on the subject. His third short novel, The Great Gatsby, was not representative; a little commercial ditty in the opened bleeding vein — a thundering condemnation of the rich — most compelling in his second novel, The Beautiful And Damned, the story of Anthony Patch, sole heir to a vast pile of wealth, far more than a thousand men could waste in a thousand lifetimes.

Anthony Patch came to luxury early in life on a small allotment of bond coupons, until his grandfather should die and make Anthony a baron of truly global rank. The elder Patch lived too long, and his estate was tied up in court for a decade, time enough for Anthony to marry, drink himself into a useless stupor, and to lose what little mind he had. THAT was the power Fitzgerald possessed, not only in subject but a truly unique writing style no one could touch, then or since.

His last novel, Tender Is The Night, took ten years to write. Wealth repulses, then attracts and destroys a youthful, charismatic medical doctor specializing in the emerging art of psychiatry. It was written with all of Fitzgerald's heartache in full focus — again, with incomparable text that no on else could begin to impersonate. I gave up trying, had to make do with far simpler work.

Some are born to write. Others do it in with blunt instruments. Hemingway was one of those, a carpenter with foolish grammar and shabby concerns. Fitzgerald gave him an introduction to Max Perkins and launched the lesser Hemingway, who subsequently ridiculed the man who gave him life. I think it made him insane and explains why Hemingway refused recognition and killed himself. He could not forgive or forget the wrong he did to far greater talent, the man who wrote "from God's point of view" as enthusiastic Fitzgerald admirers remarked. They were few, of course. Most New York critics agreed with Hemingway's sneering slander, that Fitzgerald was a Jazz Age pansy.

The Roaring 20s were unlike anything America had seen before or since, and Fitzgerald was more than a documentarian, although he had tremendous gifts of observation and rendered Naturalistic reality in all its crudity, incredibly penetrating to the ultimate meaning of it. He showed us Hollywood, New York, Paris and the Riviera, of course, but also rural Georgia and Minnesota, Switzerland, Italy, a tropical paradise ("The Offshore Pirate") and an impossibly hilarious mountain redoubt ("A Diamond As Big As The Ritz"). Many of his Saturday Evening Post stories told parables of cruelty and redemption and lost innocence.

I could have ignored it all, I suppose, but for the character of Anthony Patch — beautiful, lazy, incompetent, vain, drunken heir to an immense Wall Street fortune hoarded by a cutthroat who ruined dozens of good men. Filthy money that damned everyone who touched it. I could have ignored it, but for the power of Fitzgerald as a master of excellence.

Meh. Who needs excellence nowadays? No one alive to read it, in a world of viral pix, two sentences misspelled, tweets written by and for savages. "May Day" and "The Rich Boy" would be wasted on a modern audience, The Beautiful And Damned a boring slog from an alien time. Hamburger and pickles is plenty, thanks, munched in 16x9 with a beer and a burp.

Let's talk about Garp. Robin Williams, right? Nanu nanu!

Deployed

Oh, to be deployed again. I dream of it when I take a nap. Sleeping at night is difficult, a few hours after midnight, perhaps a couple more before dawn. Few nightmares, many dreams of deployment as an itinerant leader, a freelance director of anything. I seldom dream about directing films. Too complicated for a dream. One cannot do rocket science in a woozy state of mind, the unconscious wish to be deployed again.

I liked construction, directing men and machines, deciding how to start, little details writ in tons of rock, steep grades, the pressure of heavy loads, and deciding if danger was worth it. When possible, I worked with shovel and hammer, often to shape the result more precisely. But that wasn't my purpose. Leaders pitch in to keep others at work, confident that the boss cares enough to see and feel the work as they do, not afraid of blisters or dirt. I made them quit and rest a while, tempted them with food and water. It was a safety measure. No one was hurt. The work got done chop chop, as fast as anyone could have done it. I stretched and tied rolls of white string, did it again and again when heavy equipment tore them, boulders pinned them flat. Wonderful to see my vision prevail with a little persistence, diplomacy.

So much like filmmaking, without the pressure of excellence, a simple job. I look at the result and smile. Exactly as I hoped. Strong and smoothly graded. I saved every tree I could. Almost impossible to see the brutal war we waged, temporary power rigged, sleeping in my car each night for a month, standing guard over building materials and a trailer full of equipment, my gun on the dashboard and a PA speaker bolted to the roof rack to warn intruders. I do foolish things like that, "belts and braces" to make certain of success. Probably look silly most of the time, standing inches from a bulldozer blade to direct it, fighting with a concrete pumper hose gushing yards of stone slurry, to fill a 30-ft form I helped build for the retaining wall no one wanted, but had to be done for safety's sake, to hold the hillside together.

My dreams are a little less specific, only a feeling, something to be done with others, to deal with life on life's terms. Some nights I dream of searching a commercial building, the freight elevators and worn wooden corridors of mystery. I've seen so much of the world that I can be at ease anywhere, although I'm too old now to work at great heights, but I remember it quite clearly, rappelling from the roof of a nine-story apartment building as an experiment in my 20s. Not as easy as it sounds — and impossible now. In dreams and reality my feet are on solid ground, too old for spectacular stunts.

Never too old to direct. When my pen fails, my hands will still reach to show and tell — this way, this much, stop! A profound sense of satisfaction in leading, the only talent I was given in life.

Doesn't Matter

It doesn't matter who the President of The United States is. It could be anyone, rational or witless, qualified or not. There are several reasons why U.S. presidents don't matter.

First of all, the "Deep State" is enormous, about two million Federal bureaucrats plus two million uniformed and civilian Dept of Defense people, plus a massive cohort of 11 million state and local government workers, total 15 million, none of whom can be fired. Nor are any of them likely to resign in protest, because they all have guaranteed lifelong employment and solid gold Cadillac retirement and health benefits, swilling leisurely at a taxpayer-funded feeding trough, indif-ferent to public service or good government, enthusiastic about union rules and seniority. They do as little as possible and lie about making mistakes, which are undetectable and anonymized. Often they do absolutely nothing, because it's safe to delay, defer decisions up the chain of command, and file it with no action taken.

Because government people do very little and they have no motive to do it any better, government requires approximately 20 million contractors, including road builders, school repairs, books and netbooks, military aircraft and naval vessels of all types, small arms that every soldier and cop uses, covert operators worldwide, and above all oil suppliers and fuel transporters. Presidents can do nothing about this contractor payola, except to increase the cost by requiring contractors to hire minority employees, pay union scale, and invent total hooey like diesel from blue-green algae at $35 a gallon.

Then there's the problem of finance. No government has EVER covered their capital investment and running costs from taxation, and in today's world — forget it, no "balanced budget" on the horizon. That means selling bonds, notes, and similarly worthless paper, a 100% eco-friendly industry that produces no pollution because there are no factories or chemical effluents. It's difficult to estimate how many people are involved in selling and trading government paper, at least some tens of thousands worldwide — more if you count cleaning staff and an army of architects, steelworkers, construction contractors, furniture designers, home builders, hardware and software vendors. Presidents have little leverage in Congress to cut spending of any kind and ZERO control of finance. Whether interest rates are artificially low or tightened to get a grip on runaway inflation, Wall Street and City of London traders will multiply Treasury obligations with derivatives and "rehypothecation" that assumes nothing will fundamentally change.

Government can't default on or dishonor its obligations, except by destroying itself, which the United States cannot do. Bankruptcy of Detroit and soon the State of Illinois amp up the excitement, bailed out by our bankrupt central government, but we can't default as a nation. Russia did, but we can't. No one knows why we can't, that's all there is to it. Our economy won't function without government, it is assumed, with 35 million "public servants" and 100 million entitlement beneficiaries, $20+ trillion in debt and borrowing $1.5 million more every minute of every day. No matter who the POTUS happens to be, we can't slow the growth of Federal debt.

Foreign policy is frozen. The U.S. is hogtied in dozens of treaty alliances and sundry obligations like supplying Israel with crude oil, extending diplomatic immunity to U.N. member staff, and making nice with Mexico and Canada, our two biggest domestic trading partners. China holds about a trillion dollars of our debt and ships an infinity of consumer products to welfare recipients, retirees, school children, and every U.S. worker (roughly 40% of whose livelihood depends in whole or part on government spending). In the good old days of the 1960s, precision machine tools came from Germany. Now they come from Korea and Japan, which we are pledged to defend with aircraft carrier strike groups, hunter-killer submarines and missile bases. Why the Air Force is still flying antique B-52s is difficult to explain. B-1s were too expensive to deploy more than one squadron, and their payloads are small. It was totally tragic and stupid to retire A-10 "Warthog" close air support. Government always does that, makes terrible decisions by consensus of bureaucrats and contractors.

Domestic policy is totally out-of-bounds for a serving U.S. president, no matter who it is. No change in Social Security, Medicare, Medicaid, Food Stamps, Affirmative Action, or wholesale GSE (government sponsored enterprise) guaranteed mortgage paper that exempts banks and brokers from lending risk. The only change possible is to give away more free stuff, like Obamaphones for thugs, so they can make more efficient dope deals. Medicaid expansion is fine, but Single Payer is the wave of the future, on autopilot, just like Britain's truly terrible National Health Service. In the meantime more will be spent on VA hospitals and clinics, not less. Health insurance companies will continue to exit markets, simply shrug and give up.

Lastly, it's important to grasp that ALL government, nominally headed by a President, cannot rule anyone or anything except its own staff, for whom rules are everything. The rest of us do not give a shit about rules. We marry who we like, raise our children as we see fit, and pursue skills and abilities to exploit the world for our benefit, often in defiance of government and public opinion. Criminals numbering in millions do this with impunity. Roughly two million U.S. professionals are engaged in tax preparation, to screw government out of revenue.

President Clinton was a particularly amusing figurehead. In 1998, I wrote: "If the peace and prosperity of the entire world rests on Bill Clinton's shoulders, how does the Commander-In-Chief have time to masturbate in the Oval Office during office hours? — answer: *Peace and property don't.* Clinton's leadership is an illusion. Politicians have nothing of consequence to do, say, or decide. They are physiocratic wind-up toys, floating in a bubblebath of lukewarm hysteria, reciting platitudes written by schoolboys. We prosper to the extent that government does nothing. Clinton feels our pain, didn't inhale, and whimpers for forgiveness. If there is any justification for this carnival of hot air, it must be discerned from an abstraction, because none of the empirical data suggest any tangible benefit produced by 'sterile' public employments."

That's the bottom line on U.S. presidents, a unicorn ideal of democracy that routinely pisses off half of the electorate and, from time to time, foments murderous unrest. The Civil War was triggered and led by politicians and presidential appointees sitting as Supreme Court justices. No wonder we ignore their utterly imbecillic decrees. Liberty is the opposite of obedience.

What free people do privately matters, has real substance and meaning. What Presidents do is ceremonial and yawn-provoking for most of us, no matter how fancifully the press plays up hysterical speculation, opinion, Congressional hearings, or phone surveys. The shadowplay of White House square dancing is an expensive ornament. We could pick a President by lottery and do just as well strategically, with another lottery for Cabinet secretaries, figureheads who have no practical control of Establishment civil servants and independent agencies from coast to coast, of which 85,000 are local monopolies run by highly paid incompetents.

"In the beginning, God created school boards. This was for practice. Then He created idiots." (Mark Twain)

Fantasy fanaticism

I hitched a ride to town yesterday to pay the electric bill and to buy a carton of cigarettes, priority stuff that keeps me at the keyboard. How long I can do either is an open question. It depends on whether I can get part time work as a handyman, qualified or not.

I was quiet and thoughtful on the ride to town, trying to frame a response to war talk. I asked my elderly friend at the wheel what Bernie Sanders' foreign policy was? He and his wife were big Bernie supporters, first to "Feel The Bern" over a year ago. They bought yard signs and T-shirts and bumper stickers. If anyone knew Sen. Sanders' platform, it was my elderly Jewish friend, and he was baffled by the question. Bernie never said boo about foreign policy, as far as he knew.

Then I supposed out loud that Bernie would be too old to run again in 2020. He agreed. So, who did he think was a likely candidate to oppose Trump? What he said in reply blew my mind, the last thing I expected. He predicted that Nancy Pelosi would become Commander-In-Chief in 2019. How?? Because Mike Pence would be indicted for corruption and perjury, along with the evil, incompetent Donald Trump, and Democrats were destined to win a majority in mid-term Congressional races — which would make Pelosi the Speaker of the House again, next in line to be president when Pence and Trump were thrown in jail.

Ladies and gentlemen, I had never heard such a preposterous fantasy before in my entire life, yet it made perfect sense to a fanatic Bernie supporter. He also plays the state lottery, every week, convinced he'll win millions to "give it all away," a similarly strange idea.

I try to be realistic. Other people do it, too, including my elderly Bernie pal. When he fires up his table saw to mill another mile of nicely-shaped, very precisely cut car siding, to complete another home improvement project, he's intensely rational and reality-oriented. Never gets hurt. Always succeeds, careful to observe the quality of material, condition of saw blades, exact measurement to 1/32" tolerance. I've assisted him more than once, taking lumber from his pickup truck, handing it to him, and catching sawn pieces to stack them pending another pass on the table saw. I know for a fact that he uses reason and careful observation in every activity except political prognostication and $2 bets on winning the lottery.

Maybe I'm no different. Rational and realistic, except that I spent the last 50 years trying to do the impossible as a filmmaker, novelist and libertarian visionary out of step with the LP and orthodox Objectivism.

Perhaps a perverse insistence on heartfelt nonsense, partitioned from the common sense business of our practical lives, explains religion and similarly deliberate idiocies. I have a neighbor who talks to Seth (a dead person of considerable notoriety). She's a tarot reader who thinks that the entire Universe is a personal projection. I explained that solipsism is old hat, referred her to Bishop Berkeley. Made no impression on her. Deaf to reason, although she uses care in driving a car, succeeds in horticulture by using best practice and careful observation. Reality oriented in all things except imaginary metaphysics.

The consequences of willful fantasy in our national debate about Donald Trump are bizarre. Every day there's another barrage asserting Trump's collusion with Russia to sandbag Hillary Clinton, jigger ballots, expose Podesta's DNC emails. The fringe neo-con right is convinced that DNC staffer Seth Rich was murdered by shadowy Clinton operatives. "Arkancide" is a widely understood term in the hard money conspiracy theory crowd. I gave up on Reddit and Twitter, full to the brim with vicious goofballs. What's happening on U.S. college campuses simply beggars belief. Liberty University and BJU offer courses in "young Earth" geology, while centers of excellence from coast to coast go apeshit with antifa opposition to free speech of any kind, except Black Lives Matter, with safe transgender spaces to weep about racism, sexism, homophobia, white privilege, and sanctuary cities for serial felons.

I find myself happily pleased to read Anne Coulter, always fun to watch her in action on TV — yet she's a charismatic Christian. Ditto Pat Buchanan: tough, rational, incisive, and Catholic. It's as if the pressure of real life and rationality as a mortal animal requires a safety valve, something stupid to let us off the hook once in a while.

My personal habits are a little different than others. I spend my time fanatically fantasizing that someone on earth will listen. The contrary evidence is overwhelming, slam dunk proof. Zero book sales. No email. Cat videos and kid pix generate millions of Facebook comments, stickers, emoticons, re-posts, links, and new "friend" requests. LinkedIn is worse, a sea of salesmen and saleswomen congratulating each other for praising a brainless TED talk or a work anniversary, celebrating their servitude to something as miserable as marketing. Thought leaders on LinkedIn are a Who's Who of squeaky clean prostitutes and smiling greenies.

So. The human condition (except for nuts like me) is 90% rational, with a big safety valve to vent total nonsense, to relieve the pressure of life on life's terms. Who knows? It might be true of jihadis. They go along to get along 90% of the time — then KABOOM blow themselves up or commit suicide by cop in a gun battle. Not much different than mentally ill American mass murderers, like the bastard who shot up a midnight movie audience in Aurora. Normal people sublimate their murderous and suicidal impulses by spewing outrageous hatred at Donald Trump, or Islam, or Zionist overlords on Wall Street and at the helm of central banks and Hollywood studios. A stale crumb of debatable evidence becomes a mountain of fantasy "truth." I try to stay with the facts, as much as possible, knowing that scholarship isn't one of my strong suits.

But the reality of my intellectual life is largely fantasy, the proper realm of a filmmaker and novelist. I made a long detour into specu-lative legal theory — another unworldly dimension of romance. I do NOT recommend that anyone else follow in my footsteps. It's a steep road downhill to poverty, isolation, failure. Better to cheer pro sports and Bill Maher, praise Jesus or Karl Marx.

The Federal Monster

General Services Administration

   210,000 vehicles and 9,600 buildings, 407 million sq ft

Dept of Transportation

   69,500 bldgs and structures, plus Amtrak rolling stock

FEMA

   500,000+ temporary housing units deployed

TVA

   dams, power plants, schools, shops, 147 offices

Veterans Administration

   1,424 hospitals, clinics, nursing homes, total 9,220 bldgs

Dept of Justice

   4,200 bldgs, 70 million sq ft

USDA Forest Service

   373,000 miles of roads, 40,000 bldgs, 12,645 bridges

Dept of Energy

   National laboratories, waste dumps, 18,354 structures

US Postal Service

   33,264 facilities, unknown number of vehicles

Dept of Defense

   696,470 bldgs worldwide, plus 8 million sq ft in DC

NASA

4,660 offices and structures, 44 million sq ft

Corps of Engineers

650 dams, 12,000 miles of channel, 926 harbors, 4,000 bldgs

Dept of Agriculture

49,000 offices and bldgs, 58 million sq ft

EPA

249 offices

Homeland Security

30,725 bldgs, 48 million sq ft

Dept of State

15,743 bldgs, plus 1,200 USAID offices and warehouses

=========

Total: 912,000 structures, 3.4 billion sq ft

Jews

Sunni Maravillosa made the remark some years ago that she was "vaguely aware" of who Wolf DeVoon was, because we were both published by the same weekly webzine, along with Pierre Lemieux, Tibor Machan, Objectivist renegade Billy Beck, and many others.

I mention it because I was "vaguely aware" of who Ilana Mercer was, until I began to poke around on Facebook recently. I was delighted to discover that she has the gift of sparkling speech, and it prompted me to search for video, to hear what Mercer sounded like. She was fascinating in several respects. I felt like I had had part of my brain removed, and I'm not entirely certain that I could hold my own with Mercer in a debate. Anne Coulter? — no problem — but the mercurial rabbi's daughter from South Africa > Israel > Canada, who advertises herself as "paleolibertarian" in line with Walter Block and the Auburn mafia led by Lew Rockwell, is a force of nature as spectacular as a hot midsummer lightning storm.

I agree with much of what Ilana Mercer thinks and says in print or video. However, she made a podcast remark that went past the pale and drew blood. I don't doubt that it was offered as honest recitation of fact, but it deserves to be discussed. Explaining why all of George Bush's neocon foreign policy advisers were Jewish (Wolfowitz, Pearle, etc) the magnetic Mercer was unruffled, said that Jews held prominent roles in government and other fields because Jews are superior beings. Forgive me if I failed to quote her exactly, but Jewish superiority came through loud and clear to my simple goy ears.

As an admirer of Ayn Rand and Milton Friedman, okay, I can roll with it an inch or two. Jewish heretic Baruch Spinoza gave me a moral commandment that should be chiseled in stone: "All things noble are as difficult as they as rare."

But that's it. Everything else Jews have done in America has led to ruinous pain, especially in foreign policy, monetary policy, investment banking, psychiatry, publishing, conservative talk radio, network television, and filmed entertainment (my special area of interest).

I don't doubt that Jews are superior beings. Prof. Joseph Juhasz gaily pointed to the fact that practical engineering of atomic weapons was done entirely by Hungarian Jews — "the Chosen People," he explained. Not making it up, Joe said it to me and meant it.

Ashkenazi Jews score higher than Asians on IQ tests, top of the food chain intellectually. They are clustered in New York, Philadelphia, and Hollywood, deciding who works in showbiz, who gets published, and who doesn't. There is a pipeline from Mossad to CIA, Congress, NSC and the White House. Israel sets our foreign policy. Krugman and Krauthammer are superstars.

As a descendant of Prussian-French blockheads, I have a difficult time holding my own with sparky Jews. It took me forever to divine a simple proposition: "Justice is the armed defense of innocent liberty." Not a hope in hell it will undo the damage done by Rothbard. I've taken it on board as an unalterable truth that my work cuts no ice, sells no books, and will die when I do.

That's fine, no problem. But what the Jews did to Hollywood is unforgivable.

When will a constitution bring Leviathan to heel?

submitted to APEE

August 2, 2017

Abstract

In the United States historically and presently, the U.S. Supreme Court determines whether and to what extent the U.S. Constitution is enforced. The defect in the U.S. Constitution is political appointment of the Federal judiciary. A proposal to limit politicization was put forward by Ben Franklin at the Federal Convention of 1787. I picked it up and ran with it, as proxy member of the Governors of Laissez Faire City, a global cybernation with thousands of stakeholders that collapsed for want of common law and a constitutional judiciary.

This paper answers the question, under what conditions will liberty-preserving limitations on state agents be self-enforcing? Of necessity, I have to address constitutional design, political economy, and philosophy of law. The ideas presented in this paper reflect previous work.

In 1787-89 during contentious debate concerning ratification of the draft Constitution, it was carefully concealed that the Founders hated it, a compromise that no one wanted. Ratified, the Constitution was no longer a charter of enumerated powers, upended by "implied powers" to do anything deemed necessary or pragmatic to perpetuate and feed Leviathan. The Civil War ended federalism, voided gold clause contracts, and created monopoly railroad combinations, granting huge swathes of land through Sioux Indian Territory. U.S. Supreme Court appointees upheld slavery, conscription, perpetual union, fiat legal tender, graft, and Indian genocide.

Obviously, self-enforcing limits on state agents cannot be defined or enforced by state agents, given Leviathan's consistently evil habit of appointing obedient, intellectually quiet jurists.

Introduction

I believe it's good to begin with context. The medical condition of Leviathan is morbidly obese, a well documented fact, unable to stop eating. Less well known is the progress of freemen who chose to evade Leviathan's grasp entirely. Marc Faber is in Southeast Asia. Doug Casey has an expat project in Argentina. Sealand continues to attract capital, and the Redoubt continues to attract white middle-class refugees. It is not difficult or expensive to evade Leviathan, unless you have $250,000 income from part-time work, like Walter Block laughed about on a Mises video, or nearly double the payola, like Yaron Brook at ARI. The state knows where you live, gentlemen. The barons of Silicon Valley are monitored as carefully as hostile secret agents are. I would not be surprised to learn that Leviathan has criminal blackmail on every Third Wave executive. The revolving door between Goldman Sachs and the world's central banks is an easily illuminated feature of collusion. It is rather incredible, how big a military establishment the United States has, how much of it is in need of replacement and reinforcement.

Leviathan was and remains victorious, unstoppable except by fiscal heart attack, which seems likely at any moment. Pierre Lemieux worries that Trump will launch a war and conduct it badly — the meaning of which baffles me, since George W. Bush achieved squalor in Iraq at extremely high cost (60,000 U.S. casaulties + $2 trillion). Barack Obama's policy of defending Islam and covertly funding the "Arab Spring" created ISIS. Our political leaders are mere hood ornaments, easily changed. Leviathan is the engine propelled by general consent.

What to do with two million Defense Dept. people? or six million defense contractors and their jumbo economic footprint in real estate, retail, and stocks? Please reflect that DoD is one of the smaller claims on Leviathan's empty wallet. Government (Federal + 50 states + local) disburses four times as much borrowed money on charity and constituent bribery than on all police, fire, and military combined. The problem of fatality has nothing to do with civilian law enforcement or national defense. Obese old Leviathan is extremely vulnerable to higher interest rates. Impossibly low rates ("financial repression") has kept a morbidly frail debt junkie alive since the Tech Wreck. A sugar high of hyperinflation will kill Uncle Santa stone dead.

First Principles of Laissez Faire Law

I was privileged to be a private student of the late Gerald Mac-Callum, who gave me a single problem to solve: The rights of children. Rather than discuss every aspect of that interesting topic, here is how I answered it in fundamental law: Children have the right to be represented in court by an attorney. If a child is accused of crime or insanity, competent counsel becomes a constitutional procedural right that goes to the heart of due process and fundamental fairness. And so on, including representation in family court as a separate person with rights apart from a parent or guardian's putative privileges. In a 2003 discussion[1] concerning children, I said:

> *Children and morons have a right to be heard if they cry out within earshot of a doctor, lawyer, or extended family member. Kids and dumbbells have the right of innocent liberty from birth. Custody is not a first principle, and it is always challengeable.*

If children have a right to be represented, so too must all adults[2]

> *The right to petition and to be represented by counsel is the first and only explicit constitutional right... Due process is not an end in itself. There is a principle which*

> *logically informs due process — the presumption of innocence ("Justice is the armed defense of innocent liberty"). The most important implementation is an enduring, uninterruptable right to petition the courts...*

And to assure that legal rights are adjudicated fairly:

> *In a laissez faire community of any kind, physical or digital, the rule of law arises from and requires all of the following: a constitutional right to practice legal representation on behalf of others; the right of practicing lawyers to associate for the purpose of selecting judges who, on appointment to the bench, are barred from private legal practice; and the right of any person or organized group to obey and execute lawful orders that may be issued from time to time by the courts so created. The jurisdiction of laissez faire constitutional law and the courts which duly interpret and uphold such principles exists globally and perpetually as a matter of right. Laissez faire constitutional law flows from a single proposition, which is that no one may legally judge his own cause of action or act to penalize another without fair public trial and impartial due process of law. Laissez faire law is discovered and demonstrated in the process of litigation and trial. It cannot be legislated, codified, or imposed by a "lawgiver."* – Opinion of Counsel, Jan. 3, 2000

Political Economy

Whenever I hear the phrase "political economy" I think of Mark Twain being interrupted by a smooth talking lightning rod salesman, repeatedly upsold with premium quality twisted lightning rods and an extensive array on the roof of his Connecticut house. His essay on Political Economy couldn't be completed because of frequent interruptions. I have interrupted your awareness of the right to counsel.

Let's look at it from Leviathan's point of view.

Approximately four out of ten households are financially involved, whether as public employee or retiree, government contractor or retiree, entitlement recipient, welfare recipient, dependent, mortgage insured or affordable housing subsidized, grant recipient, DARPA researcher, or any of a thousand other protected occupations like ethanol, sugar, solar, and clergy. People vote as a bloc in favor of more government because it pays, especially tenured neocons like John Boulton and John McCain, who believe that Leviathan's first duty is to kill people and break things.

Six out of ten households are not financially involved with government, except as victims. The relationship prompts a majority of Americans to take active, thoughtful interest in how the hell we got into this horrible mess. What gives? What happened to Liberty and Justice?

They are answered with hypnotic public goods and free rider arguments. Unable to stay awake unless they change the channel, most people shrug, vote for change, and change the channel.

Therefore, Leviathan is mostly compelled to mutter to itself. Daily and weekly headlines play a loop of each mutterance, reflecting government back to itself, calming suburban Virginians and Marylanders that all's well, we need government. No need to fret. It plays well with inner city blacks, too. Centers of urban excellence like Chicago, Baltimore, Detroit, Oakland, Compton, and Camden are eager for more government money. Seattle is trying to outbid San Francisco as the most lavish local Leviathan booster, but the California High-Speed Rail project has them whipped as unimaginative pansies compared to $50 billion for track that no one needs, to join Modesto to Fresno. The cities were hoping for a couple million to repair Hwy 99, but that's the wrong mode of transport for Leviathan's shovel ready green infrastructure mandate.

Russia Russia Russia North Korea Russia China Russia. Leviathan is terribly busy, urgent top secret activity that must be investigated and overseen and hushed up for national security. We are flying B-2s over

Korea, firing on Iranian patrol boats, sanctioning Russia as a scapegoat because a phony meme about Putin "interfering" in Hillary's defeat became Newspeak.

Newspeak mesmerizes 35 million households daily. However, a Busy Majority of 200 million private sector workers are vaguely aware of Newspeak, but get distracted making a living and caring for children and elderly parents. The Busy Majority might be a receptive audience for constitutional reform, if it makes sense in a few words, and doesn't cost them anything.

<u>Constitutional Design</u>

It grieves me to relitigate the American Revolutionary War of Independence, but we must.

> *Like all liberals and most libertarians, I am forced to quote[3] Thomas Jefferson, because he did all the heavy lifting two centuries ago. Unlike my competitors, I know which epigram to recite and why it matters:*
>
> **The earth belongs in usufruct to the living; the dead can have neither power over it, nor right to it.**
>
> *Note the factual orientation here. The dead have no power to control anything. They have no right to obstruct decisions made by the living. Therefore, social settlements concluded in the past by people who are now deceased impose no obligation in the present. Presto — the right of revolution!*
>
> *It also means that the doctrine of stare decisis ("let judicial precedent stand") is basically rubbish. I appreciate that it is important to business people that law should be predictable and constant. However, it is more important to freedom that justice be understood as an evolving knowledge of truth and consequences. In*

Jefferson's time, the law of the land was monarchy. Without the right of revolution, the Declaration of Independence was logically impossible. This is the meaning of legal process—to discover justice by examining the claims of live litigants, instead of blindly applying the doctrines of dead authorities.

The mention of justice necessitates its definition, in a Preamble[4]

"Justice is the armed defense of innocent liberty."

The purposes and limitations of a first principle are: (1) to establish the context and scope of discussion; (2) to affirm the existence of a fundamental truth pertaining to the topic generally; and (3) to define that truth, employing the least ambiguous and most cognitively fruitful concepts that are logically germane to the definition. Men and women have reasoned about law for centuries. Familiar terms, the relations of which are obvious in the structure of a predicate, compel any adversary to concede or to contradict squarely, because a first principle necessarily addresses a fundamental question. The most fundamental issue in law is justice — not electoral processes or delegated powers, but the right to public justice.

Definitions of justice proffered by others have been lengthy, covering hundreds of pages, intertwining dozens of terms. However, logic is an exact science. Verbosity indicates lack of understanding or deliberate obfuscation. That's why my definition of justice is succinct. A complete theory of justice is presented in one proposition, consisting of one object, one action, and two qualifiers: Justice = armed defense of innocent liberty. The qualifiers are necessary for precision. Verbal defense of liberty isn't justice. It must be armed defense. Not all liberty, just innocent liberty (e.g., the liberty of women and children, who are often unable to defend themselves).

My definition does not refer to or imply any ethical principle. The philosophy of law is a separate branch of science, independent of ethics. Moral inquiry pertains specifically to the interests, powers, and dilemmas of an individual, epitomized by the question: "What shall I do?" Legal philosophy addresses impersonal administration of public justice, litigation among parties in dispute, the combined might of a community, and custodial guardianship of certain individuals who are unable or legally prohibited to conduct their own affairs.

Preliminary matters settled, it was fairly easy to elaborate a robust constitutional regime based on the defense of innocent liberty. Article I provides the right to petition, to sue or be sued as a private individual, A vs B, seeking common law damages or equitable reflief. Article II allows lawyers to elect judges and to pay court costs equally assessed. Article III tidies up matters of venue and juridiction. Then something wonderful happened.

It occurred to me that the right to bear arms is the source of the police power, and hence Article IV appoints and constitutes a citizen posse[5]

The right to keep and bear arms and to use reasonable force in defense of one's life and innocent liberty, or the life and liberty of another, describes the police power generally. Every person signatory to this Constitution is lawfully empowered to arrest and detain a perpetrator or willing accessory apprehended during the commission of a crime. From time to time, the Supreme Court may establish, regulate, fund, and appoint officers to an investigative agency or custodial facilities for the humane detention of persons accused of felony, and in all cases detainees must appear before a criminal magistrate within 24 hours of arrest. No accused person shall be bound over for trial unless there is actionable evidence of crime and credible testimony to establish probable cause for complaint.

The Freeman's Constitution[6] denies legal standing to fictitious "persons" such as the United States to prosecute crime or enforce legislation. Laissez faire law can't be legislated or imposed by a lawgiver. It is discovered in litigation and jury trial — not *a priori* or from a "positive" look-up table of wrongs. Leviathan does not own or operate laissez faire law.

Conclusion

I know it sounds preposterous, but there was a time in our nation's history when everything was made in U.S.A. — clothing, shoes, sporting equipment, furniture, tools, and telephones. Most people paid cash, in silver certificates or silver coin. Our government was small and solvent.

It is vain to presume that history is a one-way trap and nothing can be done to advance liberty. The way forward is simple, bring Leviathan to heel with a constitutional judiciary that he does not appoint or browbeat with endless complaints styled *U.S. v. Citizen* that seek to punish men for peaceful exercise of liberty.

I trust that Franklin's method of appointing judges will work just as he predicted, that lawyers would choose the most prosperous and respectable of their number to forsake all private clients and sit as a law judge, so that they can divide his lucrative practice amongst themselves. When courts are organized and paid for by lawyers, there will be fewer court cases and few prisons, for reasons which are explicated in depth by an ethical meditation on constitutional law.[7]

Denied the power to prosecute or punish anyone, seen as a conspiracy with a long history of robbery and criminal intent to kill people and break things, Leviathan logically lacks standing as a matter of equity. Ask your lawyer to explain what equity is.[8]

Notes

1. anti-state.com, 2003, quoted in DeVoon, *Laissez Faire Law*

2. ibid

3. op cit, pp. 65-66

4. The Freeman's Constitution, quoted op cit, pp. 166-67

5. op cit, p. 173

6. ibid

7. DeVoon, *The Constitution of Government in Galt's Gulch*

8. "The Architecture of Liberal Democracy," pp. 147-153

Marketing conundrum

Hat tip to Erik, bless him, urging me to flog my work. I explained that me and my wallet did some of that previously with debatable results. Not particularly eager to buy another $400 Kirkus review to get panned again. Throwing $300 at Ingram and another $200 at PW was a complete bust. Publishers Weekly declined to review my book, and worldwide distribution in hard cover, paperback, and EPUB sold zero copies in any format and hurt Google search. That's the reality of entry-level marketing. Serious book marketing is priced in thousands and involves hired guns. If I had the money, I'd do it.

But finally, as Erik rightly observes, it is a question of target marketing. Chris & Peachy is not for everyone, certainly not a childrens book, nor YA, nor a cosy detective mystery like Agatha Cristie. Definitely not British. No black or latino or LGBTQ heroes. Totally hot heterosexual romance with murder and mayhem, white wildcats from ruling class families, born to money and all the personal liberty and power that money confers on its children. I know something about money. I was first grandson of two moderately wealthy clans. I've met wealthy people around the world, royalty and miscellaneous multi-millionaires. My work is not for them.

Nor is it for dynamic lovers, because they are happy and don't need it.

It would be nice to reach young men, especially Marine officer candidates, serving Marines on deployment in harsh circumstances — who knows? — maybe other military men, young or old in any branch of service. Maybe they're tired of Israeli-centric assassination thrillers.

In any case, there is no money for marketing, and I refuse to spend every night making a fool of myself on social media. I do not want to walk up the learning curve of Instagram, and I don't have any enticing graphics to splash, no cat videos. What I post on Facebook is a diary, me talking to me. Five of the six people who follow me are friends, for reasons other than successful marketing. The last time I made a serious effort, I did radio interviews that sold no books. I am not my best sales representative. Fact.

Never loved?

I've been wanted, craved, needed — uniformly with buyer's remorse later — but I don't recall being loved, except perhaps by my mother. She would smile shyly and happily whenever we were together, often laughed when I smiled in reply or said something silly to amuse her.

Puzzles the heck out of me. Janet loved me, but we were only 14 and it was cloying. I was too young to be loved — excuse me, too vain and stupid, because I sent Janet away, told her that I didn't want to go steady. I believe it was the only time that a girl loved me. Had I stayed with her, my life would have been vastly different, far less crazy and reckless and idiotic — in view of which I'm glad that lovely, innocent Janet escaped my initial senseless march to perdition as a teenager that commenced shortly after I told her we were quits.

Now I'm old and unloved, too ugly to expect any tenderness. Too evil to accept expressions of good wishes or long distance warmth. I adore women, always easy for me to partner them one way or another, to the extent that they find themselves drawn. Smart ones back away, thinking of Mary Lou in particular but not uniquely. Many women are sharp enough to want money and control. I was impossible to control, chronically broke, easily bored.

For those reasons I was almost always pleased to be married. Whether I was fit to be married is a separate question. Some wives made my life easier than others, but it was never easy for them. My best behavior was in short supply, and all four wives often made uneasy sacrifices to patch me up before, during, and after a disaster or two. Queenie stuck like glue through thick and thin, until I betrayed her. Bizarrely, she still feels some sort of admiration for me, while simultaneously blowing a raspberry of ridicule, because she knows how fragile I am. "Unfit to survive," she remarked in a recent email.

True enough. I was unloved and unlovable because I'm substandard, approximately half a man. Two of me pasted together might equal a normal person. I was a major chick magnet, but women soon saw how little I could do in the world. They tried to help me, then became frustrated, worried, resentful and disgusted.

It is impossible to help an artist, fumbling his way to perdition.

Why it had to be and continues to be hell is inexplicable. In fairness to the Fair Sex, it was equally painful for men to befriend me. They learned to say little and buy me a beer, have a meal together, no further artistic or financial business to transact. I praised and encouraged everyone in my life. They seldom believed that I meant it, although it was never a lie. I knew how hard it was to create something. It was easy and natural to see goodness in others, even if they were lightyears away from me, like stars in the night sky that I enjoyed and respected. I saw hundreds of them. My life was rich with stars of stage, screen, music, science, law, and the written word — supremely talented people who achieved things I couldn't. I was a lowly director, a mere "plumber" as the bombastic Canadian producer scoffed, before he fired me. I was fired many times, humiliated in tabloids, blackballed at Warner, kneecapped by Columbia.

A failed director. Only half a man, remember?

The remnant of the half is now writing. Slight misstatement. I've been writing for as long as I can remember. Perhaps less awkwardly now, after 20 years of doing little else. Yet it's there in every breath and every dream when I sleep — the deep, unquenchable thirst to direct, to paint the screen with the talent of others in front of and behind the camera. I learned to not do technical jobs, because other men are better with cameras, sound, and editing keystrokes. The only thing I can do is to direct, and to do it, I need support staff, restaurants, hotel linen, retakes and leisure to change my mind, to see something else that asks everyone to attempt the bizarre, difficult, unlikely, often the impossible.

Now at the height of my powers, nothing has changed. Unwanted and unloved, I paint the page with the bizarre, difficult, unlikely, often the impossible and slanderous. I had to write a letter of apology to an honored friend because I lampooned the Bureau. Other friends turned two blind eyes, cheerfully bought a book that they won't read, to encourage me. Perhaps one man sees value in my work. Single digit sales are an echo of the past, films never exhibited.

Bottom line: If you have talent, any size or shape, fight for it and never quit, right or wrong, loved or unloved, until your life is ended. Artists only get one shot at life. Live as fully and freely as possible, price no object.

Reputation

Rob said something quite funny yesterday: "You'll ruin your reputation," he warned. When I saw it posted last night, it troubled me that he also said things that were ungentlemanly and cruel. I was tempted to delete it, but didn't. Friends have a right to say whatever they wish about me and the creative work I hope to pursue.

This morning after a nice sleep, decorated with interesting lucid dreams, it struck me as quite comical, a friend warning me that my reputation was in danger. Hahahaha. If anyone has a worse reputation, I'd like to know who?

Crews have called me The Guy Who Complains All The Time. Objectivists alternately sneer at me and threaten to punish. Anarchists avoid me. Libertarians think I'm stupid. My wife loudly condemned me a month ago in front of my daughter: "You're a stoner!"

Worse, I'm a chump, and I've been chumped repeatedly as long as I can remember, decades of paying too much and expecting men to remember a boon, extra cash in their hand that no one else would give and which they absolutely did not deserve. I paid too much to get a job done and then ordered workers to stop and take a break, have a free lunch I prepared. When a bore came to visit, I listened. My middle name ought to be Chump. Instead of copping a plea, I defended myself in Federal court, expecting the truth to matter, appealed pro se to the Seventh Circuit and went to prison — the smallest guy in the joint. What an idiot!

If anyone bothered to read my memoirs, any of three, they'd see in a blink that I've been a cad with women, dozens of them. I'm trying to remember a single male friend that I haven't annoyed, angered, begged for unreasonable favors and betrayed more than once.

My reputation? Hah.

Rejected by every agent, studio, distributor, editor, and publisher on earth. Smoked 400,000 cigarettes and never learned the trick of doing something popular. Kicked out of high school, flunked college courses, wrote things that made people angry and disgusted. If there is a mistake or a ridiculous blunder one can make, I've done 'em at least two or three times, learning nothing from the ordeal of deep humiliation.

Worse, I'm what Eric Hoffer called "a true believer," no better than a damn fool. I took Ayn Rand seriously, saw in her work a vision of grandeur and adventure, an invitation to dare the improbable and impossible, to think for myself.

And yet, I look at my body of work, stories and films and intellectual output that cut no ice in the market, never won me a penny of profit, no traction among "friendly" academics (some of whom I insulted, man to man, to their face in person) and it remains that I can't retract a single word, typos notwithstanding. It wasn't important to be perfect. It was imperative to be original, an unlettered clod who saw himself competent to challenge respectable people, including Ayn Rand and her faithful legions of apologists and fags.

Some months ago at a neighbor's house — extremely nice elders who I like and who have been exceptionally kind to me — it became known, grudgingly, because I don't like to discuss it, that I'm a novelist. The white haired gentleman said that he admired 'A Prayer For Owen Meany' by John Irving, the best novel he ever read. He fetched a copy, gave it to me. It was the worst rubbish ever written, #1 international bestseller, praised by Stephen King, The New York Times, Playboy, Washington Post, and Booklist. An excerpt from a Houston newspaper review was a colossal indictment of my judgment: "A long-awaited treat. This powerful story about love, faith and destiny will be placed on bookshelves and in hearts in that honorable spot right next to Garp." Pointless, awful shit, front to back, every page. When questioned by the neighbor whether I enjoyed it, I lied and said that I didn't understand it, which occasioned a long lecture. I listened and nodded my head respectfully, said little.

I should probably delete that paragraph. It's possible that he might see this post. I stupidly confessed my pen name Wolf DeVoon, and I gave his lovely wife both of my new detective novels. I dedicated 'The Tar Pit' to her and her husband, in honor of so many unearned gifts they bestowed to keep me well fed, well loved, honored, and stoned, so I could write.

That's the terrible truth about Wolf DeVoon, high maintenance, no different than a French whore. Consumed years of solitude and costly road trips, kept alive by wives and credit cards and generous neighbors, so I could write, an enterprise that paid nothing, cost everything.

My reputation in a nutshell: Hopeless romantic, patriot, a hippie who can't hold a job, never could, author of The Freeman's Constitution — ignored by the world — and worse, the author of two short detective novels, boy meets girl. They raise all sorts of hell in Los Angeles and London and Tahiti, no market for publication because they're straight white lovers.

Self-published, a millstone of shame.

If there's a lower rung of hell, I don't know what it might be, an obscure writer that no one cares to read, a failed filmmaker with no chance of directing again. Pauper. Fool. Stories unlike any other, scary celebration of heroic private liberty, armed and dangerous.

Russian hooey

Now wait just a doggone minute. I've had it up to here with Democrat bullshit. The Russians had nothing to do with downloading John Podesta's emails. That was an inside job. Testimony by Obama officials was a pack of lies, claiming that Russia attempted to crack state election tallies in ten swing states. Far more likely that Clinton contractors used proxy IPs to stage a false flag narrative. NSA knows perfectly fine whodunnit and they won't tell, because like every other Federal agency they're staffed top to bottom with Democrats.

Get it straight. The government is a Democrat plantation, 30% black and brown, the only jobs for life with Cadillac benefits that they could win on "merit" of skin color and political party. Check FEC data. Every Federal agency votes Democrat, contributes to Democrat campaigns, and takes marching orders from tenured Democrat bureaucrats and political appointees. The Federal judiciary is Democrat from sea to shining sea. LGBTQ is the law of the land, and you can go to jail for not baking them a cake. There is no such thing as an illegal alien, no matter how many crimes they commit. The only racial problem in America is "white privilege." It's a done deal, irreversible, permanent, one-party Democrat rule on both coasts.

Okay, I know a few FBI people who voted Republican and got sidelined by Democrat political appointees. Investigate Hillary Clinton or bust Loretta Lynch? — hahaha, forget it. We've been hosed. A phony dossier, paid for by Democrats, phony leaks by anonymous Obama-era staffers appointed by the most corrupt White House in U.S. history. Obama's public records were sealed, shipped to Chicago, immune from FOIA petitions. Hillary's email server was erased with BleachBit, her staff laptops and cellphones physically destroyed. Democrat consultants examined DNC server logs, to cover up who did what.

If we want to have an intelligent conversation about national security cyber threats, let's discuss Chinese hackers and spooks who go undetected, because they're clever, embedded in national security and academic institutions, at least 20,000 of them, according to Chinese sources. Fuck with us, we'll screw you, they threatened in a recent communique. Democrats don't care because Chinese donors are a durable source of campaign money and graft.

You want to believe NPR and CNN? — cool — join the crowd. Make up shit about Trump, sky's the limit. Nobody voted for him. He stole the election in collusion with Putin. He's raping the taxpayer and putting money in his pocket from ... I dunno, make something up about hotels and golf courses, or selling uranium mines (oops, wait a minute, that was Hillary). His kids are crooks, right? And he won't release his tax returns! (oops, wait a minute, IRS already leaked some of them and Trump paid the top marginal rate year after year). Impeach him! Doesn't matter why. Keep up a chant, he's unqualified, crazy, unfit to be president. Whatever.

If necessary, change the subject to global warming. Ignore global cooling in the 1970s and an exceptionally hot warming spell in the 1940s. Ignore "adjustment" of historical temperature data. Just take it on faith. NOAA and NASA wouldn't lie to us, would they? They're Democrats, Federal bureaucrats with jobs for life, and civil servants never fudge the data to get a bigger budget and fatter bonuses.

Oooo! — blame the Russians! — they're behind the disinformation about a "pause" in global warming and a slight miscalculation about hockey stick calamity predicted by Al Gore and a crackpot conspiracy at an East Anglia community college that specializes in American media studies, hands out postgrad degrees in praise of MTV cartoons and hip hop obscenities.

Go for it! Putin, Trump, Putin, Trump! Evil rich! Evil rich! Ignore the fact that all of our newly moneyed billionaires are Silicon Valley Democrats, at the head of Democrat employee PACs that top the list of Democrat campaign contributions. The top punk at Facebook wants free "single payer" socialized health care. Anyone who pays a doctor privately ought to be jailed (oops, wait a minute, top execs and pampered staff in Silicon Valley have private care and gourmet private cafeteria meals). Congress has private care and lifetime retirement payola, extra pocket money when they leave office to join the ranks of K Street lobbyists.

Putin! Trump! Global warming (oops, climate change!) Killing DNC operative Seth Rich was a robbery and they forgot to rob him. Naturally, it's an unsolved crime. Shit happens in DC. It's not like they had surveillance video or cop body cameras or dying words, right? Nobody cares if Julian Astrange offered a cash bounty to identify his killers, and he said that John Podesta's email dump didn't come from Russia. Wikileaks is a Russian black ops conspiracy even if what they publish is true. The truth doesn't matter, dipshit, it's a conspiracy theory! Er, I mean...

Putin! Trump! Climate change!

Solitaire

It's interesting that I play a "rules based" strategy with Solitaire, always turning cards from the deepest blinds, aim at winning all 52, ace to king. Most of time those rules don't work, because 97 out of 100 shuffles don't have the right distribution, or certain cards are out of sequence, wrong card at the wrong time. If I was more flexible, I'd score higher. Same thing with writing. I have certain rules that screw me as an author.

Rule #1 - Love the work. The only way to do that is to write about men and women at their best, ideal people, steady and brave and passionate, intolerant of bullshit, unafraid to be who they are. Lovers who don't give a shit about safety or security.

Rule #2 - Write the whole story without interruption, a blaze that burns for months, nothing but sandwiches and cigarettes and coffee and pot. Hammer each word on the page and never settle for the well-grooved and obvious. Ignore what other people write.

Rule #3 - Inhabit the story. Some readers complain that it's difficult to keep track of who's who in a dialogue passage, because I won't do the conventional crap — a stupifying singsong "__" I SAID and "__" SHE REPLIED. If readers can't guess from character voices and context who is speaking, to hell with them. Same thing with readers who prefer third person. If first person was good enough for Hammett and Chandler, it's good enough for DeVoon.

Rule #4 - Pay the price. I'm gambling in a racket that's rigged against me. No agent, no sales, no money to buy advertising or publicity. 18 months without income, credit cards blown to dust. No cash left to pay the electric bill. Little left to eat. One pack of cigarettes on the shelf. Persona non grata with a wife who hates me, because I've been writing 12 hours a day every day, seven days a week, instead of making money.

Those four rules are no different than Solitaire. If the cards turn just right, I win — and writing is something that doesn't win or lose on a predictable schedule. Might take years to be found at the bottom of a crowded clutter. Might be never. A few people think I can write, enough to keep me at it, to reach for the impossible, no matter whether the gamble ever pays off.

Funny encounter last night on the Objectivist Living forum. I cut off a discussion and said: "Good. I'm stupid, that settles everything." Abundantly true. I stupidly wrote what I saw in life, don't give a fuck what other people think, do, or say. I couldn't write for anyone but me and for the fictional people that I created — stubborn and stupid and dangerous lovers.

Sore all over

Sore feet, lower back muscles, hands beat up pretty bad, especially the palm on my right and several fingers chewed up from hand tools, power tools, stock. Dead tired after 18 hours in two days of carpentry. Very happy to have the work. A master carpenter gets $30/hr, a journeyman who can set a door $20. I charge $15 because novelists don't do finish work. I do rugged, square, structural shit. I built a wide 12-ft stairway and handrail in a sprawling shop formerly occupied by a pack rat, a total lunatic who collected an infinity of everything, enormous stacks of barnwood, plywood, all shapes and sizes of crap wood, about a thousand jars and coffee cans full of nails, hinges, galvanized pipe fittings, you name it, buried under piles of junk. Literally impossible to walk anywhere in a 20 x 40 two-story pig disaster. The guy has been dead four years. His sisters finally came to clean up.

So, I'm working. Next task is to rebuild the electrical system, chewed by rats, circuits going everywhere, dozens of extension cords, plug-in lights, neutral reversed several times. The cluttered workshop adjoins an equally cluttered house occupied by the dead guy's widow, a tarot reader and Windows 95 geek. Think about what that means. A Windows 95 geek.

Half a ton of shit I had to pull out and stack outside. Why a person would collect barnwood, I dunno, except as a fire hazard. Building the stairway was gratifying, not the sort of thing I do often. Made a rough estimate in my head, went to the lumber yard and loaded up 2x12, 2x8, 2x4. I had the benefit of watching real carpenters cut the stairs for our new house a couple years ago. I like to watch things happen, so I had a fair idea of what I was doing. An infinity of triangles sawn out of three 2x12s with a Skil saw. They call it a Skil saw because it takes some skill to use it. Nice stairway. Has a hinged bridge that swings down to walk into an attic over the house — indescribably filthy and rat infested, stacked with more household and farm crap. That's the next thing to attack with a P95 mask and gloves. Every wiring circuit for the house is up there, chewed.

Bank overdraft fixed. General store balance paid. I can buy electricity this month — and with a couple more days of work I might get current with Verizon and get my cellphone turned back on, although it would be cheaper to get a prepaid at WalMart. No one I like calls me, so who cares what the new number is? If I turned on the Verizon number I'd get bombarded by banks worried about something south of six figures, depending how many penalties were levied and how high the rates became for being a deadbeat. I don't care. The house has a legal moat, transferred to a trust for my daughter years ago, life tenancy for wife. All is well personally, because I don't give a fuck. I wrote Chris & Peachy. I don't care what Chase and Wells think.

I'm okay with a small town bank in the Ozarks, currently $4 to the good. If they want me another couple days, I might make it halfway through autumn. No plan to survive the winter, though. Think about it. That's how important Chris & Peachy were, two years of wrecking my credit, a fair price for such wonderful work. Novelists can be carpenters when the story is THAT good and the characters are new and distinct, never seen before. Lovers and warriors, wealthy and no fooling red hot sexy. Had to be self-published for that reason. Against the snowflake law to be straight, white, filthy rich, carry a sidearm and use it. Talk back to LAPD and FBI, laugh at them. Poor saps are hamstrung by policy and mountains of paperwork. Meanwhile, there's serious work to be done. Murder. Prison. Black ops. A sadistic serial killer loose in L.A.

So my hands are sore, so what? Chris and Peachy, price no object.

Square of Opposition

Erik asked me to explain the Square of Opposition, and I wanted to do a better job, for two reasons. The diagram I posted previously was slightly botched because I was in a hurry. It is in more exact form below. The other improvement is a clearer text explanation, as follows.

Begin with the notion that contradictions cannot exist. Something cannot exist and not exist at the same time. It cannot be all A and not A. Predicate logic (a.k.a. "classical logic") is the art of noncontradictory identification. It recognizes positive statements, negative statements, universal, and particular, organized in a matrix shown below for an important reason.

Observe that DIAGONALLY the statements are contradictory, hence only ONE of them is valid, not both. If you believe "Every proposition is true" (!) then it would be necessarily FALSE that Not every proposition is true. Of course, the greater likelihood is the reverse, that not every proposition is true. You get the same result if you consider the other pair of statements that are in diagonal opposition. We reject the notion "No proposition is true" and therefore Some proposition is true of necessity.

	Universal	Particular
Affirmative	Every proposition is true	Some proposition is true
Negative	No proposition is true	Not every proposition is true

What to do about North Korea?

1. Deploy US troops, aircraft, ships and subs

2. Economic sanctions

3. Great power diplomacy

4. Conventional war

5. Nuclear attack

We've already tried #1 and #2. Tillerson is working on #3. Pacific Command is ready for #4, long standing hired-gun payola deals with South Korea and Japan, approximately 1000 aircraft and 50,000 troops in theater equipped for conventional war, extensive satellite surveillance and tactical intel. We know perfectly well what to target in North Korea and along the DMZ.

The price of conventional war might be 100,000 dead and 500,000 wounded, mostly Korean civilians (provided that Kim doesn't launch nukes at Seoul and Tokyo, targets that he could probably hit, in which case over a million dead). We would lose several thousand US troops and a couple hundred aircraft. Absolutely certain that China would invade North Korea again. The world economy would crash. Russia may be inspired to invade Ukraine and Baltic states. No way to defuse hair-trigger animosity, panic, chaos, and global war involving India, China, Japan, Russia, Turkey, Israel, Pakistan, Poland and NATO. Conventional war in Korea is a terrible idea.

There is no "surgical strike" solution, to kill Kim and his generals.

So, how about nuclear war, low yield tactical or otherwise? I don't think the order would be obeyed. Nuclear attack requires dual authorization, the President plus Secretary of Defense, a guaranteed constitutional crisis, an immediate vote to impeach Trump. 75% of U.S. fears war with North Korea. 99% are opposed to nuclear attack. It's off the table, period.

What we're left with is a tripwire, cocked and ready to strike with everything we've got, if Kim decides to launch his arsenal in a fit of paranoia and lunacy. World history is in the hands of a single doofus. Kim cannot be deposed or appeased or talked into disarmament. I think therefore the right thing to do is to withdraw our troops from South Korea, reposition the 7th Fleet out of harm's way, tell China and Russia to deal with Kim any way they please. We gain nothing by waging another idiotic war of choice in Korea or anywhere else. The mission of American military force is to defend the United States — not Korea or Japan or Israel.

I'm not opposed to U.S. strategic nuclear supremacy, nor opposed to deploying blue-water power to enforce freedom of the seas that touch a legitimate national interest, like Panama Canal, Gulf of Mexico and Caribbean, Alaska and Hawaii, a wide margin of the Atlantic and Pacific Oceans, plus Australia, Canada and Britain, our militarily integrated, trusted kin.

It's time to let Russia and China act, with the caveat that anything they do must not touch our hemisphere or Anglo allies or despoil the planet with nuclear fallout, which we would deem an act of war against us, the only tripwire that matters. What happens in Korea is a matter for the Koreans to settle by themselves, ultimately by reunification, if China and Russia agree.

Oily bastards like Michael Medved have nothing constructive to say about this or any other aspect of U.S. national security, especially a treasonous Israel-uber-alles "world peace" fig leaf. I pray each day for freak weather to strike Medved dead in a radio studio ground fault. Among all of our enemies, foreign and domestic, no one deserves to fry more than he does. Compared to Medved, Krauthammer, Krystol, and Levin, Kim Jong Un is a toothless infant.

25,000 days

We play the cards we're dealt. I don't particularly envy anyone else's fate. One life was plenty, thanks. Slightly less than 25,000 days so far, a big inventory of adventures and disasters and modest triumphs. What else can life offer, except a spiritual treasury of wandering in the world, making decisions? Whether one wins or loses at the fabulously endowed gaming table of competition with 6 billion others, there is no alternative but to play the cards we were dealt by DNA in a place and time not of our choosing.

A body of work

Sometimes it strikes me as a massive body of work. There's a free pdf at Lulu.com, entitled Abbreviated Wolf DeVoon, 17 pages. I read it again this morning, astounded at its historic achievement in political theory, a new theory of justice. And for several days now, I've been staring at the book cover for my latest novel, Finding Flopsie, equally wonderful. If all of my works were collected in a single volume for posterity, it would fill thousands of pages. We all stand on the shoulders of giants. For me, it was Rand and RLS, Chandler and Hammett, Gene Rhodes and Scott Fitzgerald, Benjamin Franklin, James Madison, James Otis, Roscoe Pound, Frank Capra, Cecil B. DeMille, Winston Churchill, Thomas Jefferson, Abraham Lincoln, and Thomas Paine. I achieved something they did not. Quite a claim when you think about it, but true.

A novelist

- Well! - as Jack Benny used to exclaim, his trademark schtick. Each night after I cruise email and Facebook and a couple other sites that make me wonder about human competence, I've been visiting YouTube recently, high speed chases, uniformed cop valor with long lines of back-up whenever possible, plane crash reconstructions, and noir B pictures, some of which are excellent, 'D.O.A.' and 'He Walked By Night' in particular. That was fine for a while, and then I stumbled onto a clip from Blake Edwards' 'Darling Lili' with Julie Andrews. She did the most amazing strip tease I have ever seen, period. Wonderful. Absolutely wonderful.

I often bop over to Google when I become intellectually engaged in a puzzle of history, need to review crowd sourced Wikipedia. Blake Edwards wrote and directed hundreds of movies and TV episodes, all of it quite brilliant. Big pictures like 'Operation Petticoat' and 'The Great Race' plus the truly fabulous Pink Panther pix with Peter Sellers as Inspector Clousseau, 'Victor Victoria' with Julie Andrews, Robert Preston and Jim Garner, and '10' with Dudley Moore. His lifelong collaboration with Henry Mancini began with the Peter Gunn detective series that ran for three seasons, after a hugely successful network radio series 'Richard Diamond' starring Dick Powell. Of all the modern directors, Blake Edwards was a genius, more decency and good humor than anyone else, a simple, stunning fact, rewarded with boffo box office.

Big deep breath. Blake Edwards grew up in Hollywood, started as a teenage actor, had family and friends in show business, plenty of opportunity to shine, everything I did not have as an outsider wannabe from Wisconsin. By the time I got to Hollywood in 1980, the studios had sold their back lots, their money-losing sound stages, and their classic film libraries long ago. Show business was mired in recession, no new talent wanted behind the camera. Blake Edwards moved to Europe, made money doing his Pink Panther pix, and he skewered Tinsel Town as a snakepit of churlish, incompetent assholes in 'S.O.B.' -- an unbelievably wicked satire, if you haven't seen it. Everything Blake Edwards touched turned to cinematic gold.

Bottom line, I'm too old to make movies, too late now. Never really had a shot at it, however talented I might have been as a film director. Google says that I'm a novelist, not something I wanted to do in life, but last night I finally accepted it. There's another book already outlined, and it simply makes sense to go back to work as a writer, do what I've been given in life. I can't be Blake Edwards, but I can do something he didn't, paint with vivid language on the page, gracefully surrender the things of youth and be the mature, confident storyteller I am.

UPDATE: the book I outlined is nearly completed, Finding Flopsie, easily my best work. It cost quite a lot personally. My future is opaque. Why it has to be this way is baffling but familiar, villified and unrecognized. When I was shunned by Hollywood, I shrugged and began to write fiction. To be so completely frozen out as an author is mysteriously suggestive. Perhaps I was a better filmmaker than I was willing to admit, pushed aside for reasons that perhaps have little to do with time or place or medium, uniform rejection of everything and anything I create.

All the shit I've done to people

I've been watching a video I made yesterday, a compilation of film footage and still photos, highlights of my career as a showman. I should say sadistic lunatic. A truly incredible list of crimes. I threw pies in people's faces, dumped buckets of paint on their heads, made them slip and fall, set them on fire, had a dwarf use a slingshot to shoot a marble at a showgirl's butt on stage. I forced a perfectly respectable, capable cinematographer to use a single bare lightbulb in a ceiling fixture. I bellowed at a dignified senior producer in a swish West End restaurant and demanded a four man crew, two cameras instead of one, and when I got to the concert, I bullied and berated the group's manager to let my people walk on stage with the headliner. I've told people to their faces that they had no talent, give it up, don't even try. The number and depth of my egregious financial sins were too many to count or weigh.

I've been incredibly cruel to women in intimate circumstances, demanded pregnancy, threw away their innocence and dignity, sent them through studio gates to deliver a screenplay, dress for maximum pleasure, watch me flirt with another chick.

Some of my stunts were preposterously vain, challenging top executives who had the power to crush me. I routinely manipulated friends and colleagues, family members, decent folks who admired me and wished me success. I think I drove my father insane with distress and shame. I was snotty with a Federal district judge and forced his hand two or three times. I told a distinguished, well known philosopher that he was full of shit in front of other guests on my patio. "I've written twenty-two books!" he bellowed in rage. I laughed him.

Worse, much worse, I think that some hundreds of people, maybe thousands were moved by ideas that I promulgated. I put my hand on the lever of history. No sense of humility.

I hope and trust that I'm nearing the end of life, alone and shunned for ample cause, which is more or less fair and square. You know what I learned? I'm a fucking idiot, not to be trusted with a bag of chocolate donuts and cheese and onion sandwiches. No sense of restraint. We get exactly what we deserve in the bathroom at 4 o'clock in the morning.

OMFG, I just remembered! In a 1982 filmed comedy sketch, I had a bad tempered dinner patron at a fake restaurant berate a young black waiter, grab him by the necktie and shove his face in a bowl of cold noodle soup. "Okay, I'll heat it up right away, sir," he begged contritely with noodles hanging off his fake mustache. The title of the sketch was Winning Through Viciousness. I didn't write it, but I staged it and directed it. The black kid did a brilliant job, and I was astounded, exclaimed to my cast and crew how brave an actor he was.

People always did as I asked, high and low, around the world. I've called doctors to come in the middle of the night to sew up an attempted suicide off the record, Russian bodyguards to assault a village at dawn. I persuaded traffic cops to let me go after chasing me for miles.

Jeez. What a long strange trip it's been, made a million mistakes, published a million words, took a million liberties in the name of art, the highest form of pleasure known to man. I faced killers and aristocrats and people who were eleven times smarter than I was, held my own, bent them to my purpose or told them to fuck off.

Why? -- because we live but once. I lived.

An alternate universe

I often wished I could have had a respectable life like Scott, heir to a foundry, solid citizen. Last time I saw him, he was mowing his lawn, smoking a cigar, grumpy as heck. Something similar happened to Glen, sad and truculent. Cheerful, cute Joette died young. Eileen became an academic feminist, a functionary of government. Tootie played well with others, smiled a lot. Tommy was a naval officer. Steve followed in his father's footsteps, a bank officer. He was stuffy and unhelpful when I helped my mother present a check to pay off her mortgage. Probably got fired when his small town bank was acquired by a regional brand. Up or out, right, Steve?

Charlie became a librarian or something at an ashram, after a long career as a drunk. My pal Tom worked at the same part-time job 30 years with occasional forays in video, much of it access comedy, old jokes told twice. Jay faked reality and used Ronco Spray-On Hair. I didn't think he was particularly talented or clever, but Jay lived his entire life in show business and did a great job as art director on a show that Tom produced and I directed in 1982.

Okay, suppose I had been born in another time, like my father. He drove a halftrack in WWII, went to college and met my mother. Five sons used him up, kept him indentured to a job and a small town that he hated, beaten into accepting Food Stamps, devastating humiliation. He always wanted to work construction, move to Arizona, got to do neither, died where he was born. Ditto Uncle Fred, a bachelor shunned and shamed by pilfering a client's cash, did tax returns for helpless idiots, died in the house that he and Aunt Mary inherited, never left the nest. My brothers fared okay, I guess. Roger did exceptionally well, but he was hobbled by caring for my parents in their long horror of illness and incompetence. I escaped and never went back, except to visit and

escape again as quickly as possible. There was nothing for me in Mil-
waukee or the crushingly airless German village that destroyed my
parents.

Lemme think, who do I admire? Anne Coulter for sure, Ivy League
law school, happy as a clam and perfectly confident no matter how
awful the opposition. She laughs at them. Margaret Thatcher was
wonderful in the same way, tough, happy, skewered blockheads gaily
and took down the Soviet Union in partnership with Reagan. I did not
want to be Ronald Reagan, nor did I admire Donald Trump. George W.
Bush was a stone idiot, his father equally shallow and conventional. Jeb
is the smart one? Hahahaha.

Oh, come on, surely there must be someone who you'd rather be?

Blank stare. Hammett and Chandler had horrible lives, Fitzgerald
infinitely worse. Patton was a monster, although George C. Scott was
splendid. It's certain that Jimmy Stewart was loved, but I'm not sure
how good an actor he was. Acting was unnatural to me, directing
automatic. That was the only definite talent I exhibited as a kid —
ringleader, organizer, leader. A client in Philadelphia asked: "How long
have you been an idea man?" The question stunned me, made me
think, and the only thing I could say was: "All my life."

That's good news and awful news. In a recent email, my brother
Roger opined that I was a "visionary," which was a respectable office
on occasion (Edison, Voltaire, Grotius) but more often a trainwreck:
Marx, Jesus, Mohammed, Kant, Owen, Wilson, FDR, Mao. I like to think
that I advanced better ideas, but the price was awfully fucking steep,
an entire lifetime and big misadventures to discern a simple idea or
two. I never regarded myself as particularly talented, aside from directing and editing, storytelling.

Denied a career in show business and exiled as an author, I should
have done something else in life, but what? Butcher, baker, candlestick
maker. Machinist, artist, janitor. But the truth is inescapable, I was
always a terrible employee. Personal best was a year at Disney, pushing
paper and pushing the envelope, unwanted. I was under a lot of pressure. Tab Murphy had adapted Hunchback of Notre Dame, a one-sheet

poster opposite my cubicle, saw it ten times a day. Tab got a nice six figure WGA payday and I got $15 an hour to master Miramax bullshit. We started out as apartment neighbors in a cheap North Hollywood lanai. Cut it out, quit bitching. You don't want Tab's karma, nor Tarantino's or Spielberg's, that's for damn sure.

Okay, more truthiness, I was horrible at math. I remember the classrooms quite clearly, 14 years old, totally lost in geometry and pre-algebra. No science for you, dumbshit. The specific alternate universe I hoped for as a kid was radio communications. I couldn't memorize Morse Code to get a ham licence, a cognitive deficit, every second a new blank slate. No wonder I needed help as a filmmaker, couldn't shoot my own stuff, had to be prompted by a script girl on the set, made silly mistakes and missed common sense visual opportunities, emotionally overwhelmed by a performance, a stunt, a dolly move, a moment of life in high relief.

Sex mad, moment by moment seduction in high key. All I can do is shake my head, partly in plain disbelief. Gone now, of course. Too old and feeble to fuck. So I started putting porn on the page, outrageously graphic. No wonder I write so slowly. Stories unfold in slow motion, unplanned and extemporaneous. Plain language. A deep seated fear of repeating myself, using the same word or same idea twice, an impossible mission. Unread, utterly isolated.

Poop. Happy to be me, with one simple misery, grinding poverty, unable to feed myself. The draw of an alternate universe is money, applause, recognition as an idea man. Too late now. My ideas were unwelcome. Is that the fate of all visionaries? Terrible result.

Or is it? Consider Kavanaugh. Silver spoon, only child, first in his class, athlete, Yale law school, secret White House clearance, Harvard law professor, circuit court judge, never thought a radical idea in his life, squeaky clean follower of fascism, suddenly ruined by black ops, another turn of the torture screws every day and every sleepless night. He will die a broken man, a straight-laced Boy Scout eaten by the lions. Compared to Kavanaugh, being me sounds pretty good.

An awkward situation

If you don't hear from me via Blogger or Facebook or email periodically, I probably died.

No reason not to die. I wrote to Brigid a couple weeks ago and said that I don't have anything further to reach for or achieve, not after Partners, which is true.

I settled a trust, made a will and a full disclosure in print if my daughter cares to re-examine who her father was. It would be nice to pay off my account at the general store, but frankly it won't be much of a crisis for anyone if I die a pauper. My brother Roger will grumble that I owe him $60, but Chase and Wells Fargo can go climb a rope, for all I care. An executive at Gulf + Western once told me not to worry about debt, after which it was easier to move forward as a film director.

The world has had multiple opportunities to advance my creative career, fifty years worth of movies and books and essays. I got nada. I'd rather not talk about the bullshit they preferred. We each take a turn at the spinning wheel. What goes up must come down. Of all the music I loved, Blood Sweat & Tears moved me like no other. Sorry, Frank.

Since I'm talking about death, here's my playlist for a memorial:

21st Century Schizoid Man, King Crimson

Talk To Me Darling, The Pretenders

In The Light, Led Zeppelin

Nights On Broadway, The Bee Gees

My Little Suzy, Styx

Spinning Wheel, Blood Sweat & Tears

Sofa #2, Zappa

It's on my mind because I fainted and fell down flat on my face in broad daylight, rearranged some ribs and bruised a number of muscle groups, had to use pain pills for 10 days, couldn't cough or sneeze without howling. Better now, but vulnerable, no longer strong enough to do serious labor. My brain still works, although 400,000 cigarettes and family history make me a good candidate for stroke or heart attack. Occasionally I wish to die. Impossible to kill myself, because it would hurt my daughter, which I cannot entertain, absolutely verboten. I have to die from natural causes. So I wait patiently.

Doo bee doo bee doo.

An outgoing personality

Hmph. Explains everything. I'm shy, stammer in public, seldom speak to people who I know personally or professionally, although I'm a good listener and I laugh easily.

Talking might be a genetic deficit. I have no recollection of my father or mother speaking. Uncle Fred was silent. The only photograph of my grandfather showed him deep in thought, standing with a more animated (i.e., normal) person. My daughter is silent, too, unless she sings to herself in a remarkably singular style that's uniquely her own, perfect pitch without lyrics, a truly lovely creative warble. She's physically elegant, a natural dancer like I am.

From time to time I speak aloud to myself, addressing a big crowd in full voice, walking by myself, as if there's a deep unfulfilled yearning to speak because I have so much to say. No doubt that's why I write, tongue tied in public. It also explains why directing movies was nearly impossible. My orders on the set were often terse, impersonal. I was silent and stupid when I was interviewed for All Things Considered.

My fictional male characters don't say much, either, but they have rich internal monologues full of thought, capable of spontaneous deception or comic quips. I sometimes surprise folks with penetrating observations. It's hell to be smart and to see the deeper context, embarrassing to name it, no talent for diplomacy. It disqualified me from normal employment, forces me to live alone.

What's most bizarre of all is that I'm affectionate, generous, glad to be alive and happy to witness every manner of human and animal life on earth. I talk to cows, dogs, birds, bunnies, strangers, children, cops, lawyers, doctors, hillbillies, and shopkeepers, provided that I don't have to discuss serious ideas, unable to say what I really think.

It grieves me to edit what I say in print.

In a crisis 20 years ago, commemorated in Walking To Ayrshire, it was imperative to find an explanation for my silence and isolation, so I looked on the web and saw myself described as a victim of Asperger's Syndrome. On my first visit to a clinical psychologist, I told him, and he categorically dismissed it as rubbish. There was nothing wrong with my mind or personality. Five years later, I received an unsolicited email from him, said he was amazed that my "star was shining so brightly" as the author of The Freeman's Constitution. No other man on earth has recognized it as an achievement, defining a new theory of justice.

So, I'm silent, isolated, impoverished, incapable of small talk, shunned by the organized world (except for a Scottish shrink) because what I think and worked hard to create is unwanted.

Anywhere, maybe nowhere

"Where to, bud?" the taxi driver asks cheerfully.

Imaginary dialogue that happens every few minutes. I have nowhere to go. My dog was run over by a FedEx van barreling down the hill yesterday, swerved to straddle him laying in the middle of the road on a sunny day. I called Tooie out of the road hundreds of times, made him sit and stay out of harm's way. Old shihtzus don't listen, have their own agenda. He's up at the house, broken foreleg and internal injuries, laying quietly on bathroom tile, stoned on doggie pain pills left over from oral surgery a couple years ago. Took all the pleasure out of life, as you may perhaps understand if you ever loved a dog. He was at my side day and night for nine years, slept at my feet in bed each night, rescued from a shelter at age three or four. Not knowing if he would survive, I dug a grave yesterday. Enough about that.

The prospect of losing Tooie was the last straw. Six weeks ago, I collapsed face down in the dirt in broad daylight, couldn't move, had to crawl. It left me enfeebled and now I use a hardwood cane, especially going uphill at a half stride, or is it a quarter? A slow shuffle, nothing like my emphatic stomp as a younger man, raising hell around the world before I turned 40, doing it again in my 50s, all six continents, and plugging along in my 60s to wage war with philistines, to buy property and build a house. Impossible to go further now. No money, no car, no stamina. I used myself up, every ounce of brain and muscle.

"Where to, bud?"

Well, it won't be writing another novel. I know what they cost. It won't be another movie, strictly a young man's game. It won't be a tech project. No imagination. Too old and ugly to grin, unqualified and inept as a salesman or preacher.

I said everything I hoped and wanted to say. Now it's the world's turn to do something about it, discover merit in my ideas and literary legacy. I won't hold my breath. The world has other things to do, like honor more negroes, kill fossil fuels, and impeach Donald Trump. My work was shunned and ignored. No book sales. No film rights sold.

"Where to, bud?"

I don't know. I have a few years left, perhaps, no desire to visit Wisconsin or California, and I couldn't buy a plane ticket or rent a car if I wanted to. Credit cards vaporized over a year ago, no cash in hand, $15 in my checking account, just enough to keep it open. It's a free checking account for senior citizens, no monthly fee. When I tore up the forest and built a house, I ran tens of thousands through it, six figures through company accounts at Chase and Wells Fargo and Frost and a bullion account at the Perth Mint. All balances zero, company defunct, probably in trouble with the IRS. The last time I filed a tax return was in 2015.

"Where to, bud?"

I don't know. Anywhere. Maybe nowhere, to die in my sleep from boredom and want. I've been postponing it as long as I could, pushed myself to write a masterpiece, kept going until I was convinced that it had been achieved in July, two months ago. I collapsed and fell down a couple weeks later, took a long time to get back on my feet. Then my dog got hit by a van. I don't think that my daughter needs me any more. All grown up, headed to college.

No strength to stand on my feet part time at a McDonalds, flipping burgers. No brain to run a complicated digital cash register. No mountain left to climb. For the first time in my life, I'm finished.

Not beaten — I carved my own way, forded raging rivers of opposition, an ocean of cowardice and despair. Certain achievements stand out in particular, like the preamble of The Freeman's Constitution, a new robust definition of justice. Whatever happens next is okay in that respect. I hammered a legacy on Earth.

The imbecile folly of legislation

It happens like clockwork, almost hourly. A thoughtful citizen calls a talkradio show. "Why can't Donald Trump raise the money he needs for a wall from private contributions?" — and the radio host replies: "You can't spend money like that without legislation."

Hahahahahaha. Nailed it!

Can't do anything without legislation? That's what's wrong with America in a nutshell. All it takes is one Senator to block a bill or confirmation of an appointment, a couple dozen in the House to block something as urgent as a border fence to keep out another 100,000 migrants who are gathering in more mass caravans to be caught and released to get free food, housing, and health care, because Democrats want to increase the number of California congressional seats based on population, giving them more legislative power, as if lawmaking will make MS-13 or anyone else on the wrong side of the law behave like Girl Scouts. Maybe Chicago needs more laws against murder, illiteracy, and "knock-out" assaults on white people. What legislators normally do, of course, is to throw more money at problems created by previous bonehead legislation. The only thing they know how to do is to make government larger and more expensive, sometimes at a gallop. Bush blew $2 trillion invading and occupying Iraq. Congress let him do it.

Look at any of them individually, Federal lawmakers from either party. I don't know which is worse: morons like Maxine Waters and Sheila Jackson Lee, or liars like Nancy Pelosi and Dianne Feinstein. The Republicans are no better. Remember lame-duck Flake caving in the Kavanaugh hearings, requiring him to be smeared and humiliated? How about Michelle Bachmann performing fallatio on a big corn dog at the Iowa State Fair. Or McCain killing repeal of Obamacare.

Don't blame politicians. The problem is legislation.

If you unwind American history, what you see is a long series of constitutional blunders, all the way back to the Massachusetts Bay Company, earliest example of self-government as a legislative body led by lunatics. It was a chartered enterprise that escaped Parliament and Royal control by exploiting a loophole in English law. They sat as shareholders and voted to purchase African slaves, to capture Indians to swap for more slaves, and to banish anyone who had an independent idea. (That's how Connecticut and Rhode Island were born.)

Farther south, the enlightened Maryland Toleration Act was hilarious. Catholics would do business with other sects, but atheists would be put to death.

You would think that with all of our colonial outrage about The Intolerable Acts, The Townsend Act, and the adamant refusal of Parliament to listen to reason, it might have dawned on us that legislation was a lousy idea — but the tenor of the times was solidarity and self-defense as a free people of planters and tradesmen (not including slaves or Indians, of course). War with England necessitated cooperation in Congress and shared sacrifice. All well and good, until the bill for the Declaration of Independence came due. Suddenly, we were at each other's throats, refusing to pay war debts and taxing each other's produce like foreign states. New Jersey was compared to a cask tapped at both ends, taxed by New York and Pennsylvania, myopic state legislators in full panic, struggling to get their financial noses above water.

After a misfire in Annapolis organized by Madison and Hamilton, the states sent delegates to Philadelphia. Two months of squabbling cobbled a compromise that no one liked. Franklin begged them to sign it, warts and all, because failure would cripple united, urgently needed action to resolve border disputes, bankrupt state and Continental treasuries, and radically divergent ideas about slavery. Delegates must NOT report failure. Act now before the states break into two or more rival confederacies, which some parties had openly threatened.

Conventions would ratify or reject the compromise.

Virginia and New York, the two most populous and prosperous states, were alarmed and repulsed by the idea of yielding power to a new government. Madison and Hamilton wrote a series of articles to sway public opinion, aimed primarily at New York electors. Federalist and Anti-Federalist roared at each other on public platforms and on paper. Ultimately, New York voted 30-27 to ratify, an extremely thin margin of TWO swing votes that might have killed the Constitution stone dead. In Virginia, the tally was 89-79 to ratify, an equally angry division between those who saw an opportunity to advance as U.S. legislators and others who defiantly refused to yield state sovereignty. There were prominent Virginians on both sides of the question, and the 47% who were defeated by Madison were extremely pissed off. Jefferson was in Paris, Patrick Henry led the opposition.

We went through the agony of pissing people off almost every year of U.S. history. Lincoln was elected U.S. President by 39% of the popular vote. No wonder we had a Civil War, with 600,000 dead and injured, the Southern and border states destroyed, conscription riots in Wisconsin, and Federal bankruptcy papered over with worthless "greenbacks." Gold loans and U.S. common law were sweepingly abolished by a politicized Supreme Court decision. Previous Supreme Court decisions held that African slavery was a natural condition and that Indian tribes were in a permanent state of pupilage, no right to property, treaties notwithstanding. Cue the Souix, Crow, Comanche, and Apache war parties.

We have a long history of pissing people off, legislating ourselves into penury as an idiotic bipartisan war vote, or winner take all by a slim margin, appointing Supreme Court judges who are little more than politicians in black robes. I refuse to call them "justices."

Such lack of imagination! — copying everything that we despised about the limey Parliament and prerogatives of royal Divine Right. Electing citizen U.S. presidents changed nothing. We cut our throats repeatedly, voting to elevate aristocrats, populists, war heroes, and community organizers with vague, elastic powers, no different than a king. Franklin Roosevelt ruled for 13 years and imposed socialism as national economic policy that would never be revisited or challenged, only amplified and extended and multiplied, no matter which party was in power. Mandatory entitlement spending is currently 2/3 of the Federal budget. Federal agencies are holding trillions in mortgage paper, "troubled assets," export guarantees, SBA loans, student loans, GM bailout paper, GSA inventories, Amtrak rolling stock, space probes, physics laboratories, reactors, gigantic waste dumps ...

So sad. We blew a chance to figure it out, perceive that voting and legislation is unending farce. Now we're in the deepest ditch possible, no way out, $25 trillion in debt, hordes at the border, legislators at each other's throats again, incompetent to do anything except hurl insults at each other and smear a duly-elected president, fighting over another Supreme Court and an elderly, highly political "justice" who's dying, dead, or comatose. Don't kid yourself. The campaign to impeach Trump (and then Pence) is a Deep State covert operation to stop him from choosing another Supreme Court nominee who might think independently and change something.

There are constitutional alternatives, but America is deaf, proudly clinging to your right to vote legislative disaster after disaster, pissing off your neighbors, tussling over spoils that are nothing more than promises to make our innocent progeny pay in the future.

Awkward anarchy

It's right in my face this morning, like a bad car crash, that I gambled recklessly and lost. The situation is of deep significance to no one other than myself. It would be different if I was young and pretty and innocent. Women and children are forgiven easily, authors never. An injured dog has a better chance of winning shelter and sympathy.

Elderly neighbors took in a starving stray, fed her, paid for vet care, spent thousands of hours to bond and win grudging obedience measured in seconds, as in one or two, after much pointless shouting. The same elderly couple have kept me alive during the last two years with pound cake and cookies, terrible but servicable leaf to help me face a blank page. The power utility is less generous and grocery stores can't compromise their business survival to aid a nonprofit enterprise. From time to time I think about county welfare or disability. I'm too old for crime and I'd rather not go to prison again. Once was plenty.

I often wonder about my sanity. These words will go unread, like my latest novel will, after months of daily struggle to glimpse a preposterous story, one scene at a time, each moment of their fictional lives blown from sparks to a roaring blaze. There is a terrible sadness when a novel is completed. Not a word can be altered. I suspect that's what prompts me to create new work, however sincerely I wish to quit the journey -- and must! -- if I'm to survive.

I often wish to die, happy with my body of work, some dozen or so titles self-published and ignored. A new theory of justice, likewise ignored. My creative arc crested long ago. What I have been writing the last two years are stories no one can possibly enjoy, except myself. The embarrassment is easily explained. I'm writing what I can.

Simpletons think simple thoughts. Courage matters, resistance to tyranny a costly job that few undertake. Romantic love and sex are the greatest wonders of all. It pains me to see retail amusements, a pretense of happiness that's little more than a fake sun pasted on a blackened sky. I feel sorry for millions, tens and hundreds of millions, billions of people who have nothing else. Every moment of their youth and yearning is to be celebrated, however they can and however they must, in the confines of a unchosen time and place, an animality of tuneless incompetence, owned by pop stars, advertisers, boss, in-laws and neighbors. Their destiny is to suffer the worst of evils -- a Stephen King gargoyle to terrify them, give them nightmares transmuted into giddy laughter, something to talk about.

People of dignity never speak. They see and understand. Their words are a treasure, seldom squandered. Not exactly hoarded, but neither thrown like vomit or free coupons of watery social concordance to smooth the feathers of emotional chickens. My wife keeps chickens, so it's a ready metaphor. They come for food and shelter, flee everything else, helpless at night in a stupor of irresistible roost. If you want to chop a chicken's head off, it's easier after dark. That's the murderous trick that Stephen King employs. You are alone in a darkened theater, in a stupor of attendance, unable to resist. Literary victims read King's books alone at night.

Well... there's a cheery thought, I can't give anyone nightmares, because I'm unpopular to extinction, unread. In an upbeat mood I sometimes feel deliberately shunned, because my heroes are white and manly, the heroines lovely and brilliant, equally courageous. There are tens of thousands of more amusing authors, although I'm damned if I can find any. People often suggest a book, thinking it would improve my mood or widen my eyes. They don't see who I am. All my life I have avoided successful popular films, because I was a filmmaker. Its hard to read bestselling authors. Three pages are enough to disgust me.

So, I write what I can, just as I once made the films that I could. There is a commonality and symmetry of directing a movie and writing a novel, the same focus, heavy lifting of inertia, hammering it ruthlessly, relentlessly, cheerfully until it shines, original work worth doing. How did Jefferson say it? - a decent regard for a candid world, or something like that. My novels are a love letter to the unborn, a future progeny in search of inspiration, those who are unwilling to poison themselves with King and Tarantino and South Park.

How to befriend yourself

(1) Acknowledge that you would not need to befriend yourself unless you were otherwise friendless and had fucked up badly enough to be forgiven by someone, even if it has to be yourself.

(2) It is the human condition to live a life not of our choosing. We make grievous mistakes and rash decisions. If you're friendless, obviously you have fucked up big time.

(3) Let it go. There is no shame in living, however poorly organized, uncompensated and culpable. Rejoice in the fact that you made it this far.

(4) Crime is always debatable, a fuzzy line blurred by duty and destiny. Killing in uniform doesn't make it right automatically. If you've injured others (who hasn't?) take comfort in the knowledge that you were injured, too, at a minimum by self-inflicted suffering.

(5) Befriending yourself has to be real and mean something, not just a "piecrust promise" subject to cancellation. The deepest heart of life must say to yourself what a grand gift life is, and it's your life to live, life on life's terms.

Unwanted outcomes are commonplace, so befriend yourself, son, there may be worse to come.

A private letter

Hi.

No particular reason to write to you, except the pleasure of it. I haven't looked at _____ recently, a little shy of it because you're going through a difficult passage. I'm reluctant to say anything else, except the sincerity of how lovely your heart is.

I think the world of you. Tough and tender and wise. Your jokes are always surprising (and funny). Your photography is always original and highly evocative. Humming along in the background is the flinty, competent warrior who I admire. If I haven't mentioned it recently, I'm sheepishly grateful for the protection your kind bestows on softer, less qualified civilians like me. Hard to grasp that there are only a million sworn LEOs to police 330 million. If you do the math, it works out to less than one cop on duty per thousand sitting ducks. Absolutely vital for women to learn how to shoot, use good judgment about situational awareness, and so forth. You've done a splendid job of making firearms a simple, straightforward matter of study and training, showed them a logical assortment of handguns, weighed pros and cons in accessible language. Separately, I've always admired your literary prose, the scope of your view, earthy and realistic and often transcedant.

There should be a law against long paragraphs like that. Sorry.

It's quite marvelous that I was able to write Partners. Thanks for seeing that Kyle has a sense of honor and aspires to do right, as strange and cold as his circumstances may be. He's a surrogate for all ordinary men who are incapable of remaking the world, have so few choices, saving himself to the extent that he can, unwilling to sell himself cheaply, let his life slip away into meaningless ennui. More talented and less talented men don't struggle with Kyle's anguish. He's no different than Chris Cable, except that Cable was Ivy League, came from a honored tradition of military service and grave responsibilities for national security. Slightly absurd of me to create such a figure, knowing so little about the real men and women who serve in uniform. I took it as elemental that grisly combat is a heavy burden, based on observations I made, troubled vets and twisted survivors of clandestine ops. Forgive me if I misrepresented various agencies and took ludicrous liberties as a storyteller. I wasn't interested in Cable as a character so much as a narrator, a plausible foil for Peachy. I ought to be ashamed of myself for making Mary Blount an adolescent boy's ideal fantasy babe. Writing should be a licensed profession.

No particular reason to blather about my tawdry concerns, although I'm humbled by all the support you gave me. It sustained me in long dark hours and made it possible to be the best novelist I could be, such as it was. I have nothing else to write, that's my sense of it, nothing left undone or yet to attempt. Not after Partners. Thank you a thousandfold.

Aw, jeez

Sebastian Gorka was given the Medved slot on Salem. He decided to call his show 'America First.' What does he talk about daily? Israel. You'd think that a former Trump adviser would have the stones to do the right thing and call it 'Israel First,' a dollop of plain speaking.

Truly incredible how many hours a week we're hounded by neo-con Zionists, no mention of how many trillions and how many American lives have been thrown away in service to the Jewish State. Invasion of Iraq was to defend Israel. Hammering Iran economically is to punish them for supporting Hezbollah and Hamas. 40,000 U.S. troops and sailors are based in Kuwait and Bahrain to protect Israel. $3 billion a year in foreign aid cash and tens of billions in U.S. weapons were handed to Israel; an equal amount of aid propped up Egyptian dictators to keep Gaza fenced like a prison. Syria was smashed to defend Israel. Our decades-long U.S. guarantee supplies Israel with crude oil and blocks Security Council action. Half of Israel's settlers who seized more land from Arabs were American Jews. U.S. Jews privately send $2 billion a year to Israel, every kid in America is hectored about the Holocaust, and an Israeli was funded with tens of billions of U.S. and California subsidies to build uneconomic electric muscle cars, solar farms, and "private" rocket failures that were launched on NASA's dime.

It's difficult to exaggerate how powerful The Tribe is.

NPR, The New York Times, CNN, Bloomberg, Facebook, book publishing, comic books, Broadway shows, music publishing, actors, agents, studio executives, movie distributors, Wall Street investment banks, Treasury and DOJ officials, powerful U.S. Senators and Supreme Court justices. Guess who owns Fox News.

Not good enough for Mark Levin, of course. He demands hand-on-heart fealty to Israel from all U.S. politicians, all U.S. media outlets and all U.S. citizens in perpetuity, no matter what the Jews did, do, or might do, past, present, and future. He wants us to pledge U.S. military power to destroy Tehran and Damascus, because God gave a nomadic tribe of former slaves the eternal and exclusive right of conquest.

Pt-t-t-th.

Cards dealt

I've been sitting here stewing, playing Solitaire, thinking: Well, shit, I'm playing the cards I was dealt. I'm the world's worst novelist, too bad. Other people are crippled, stupid, doing an exhausting job they hate, or hopelessly shy, stuck in Tehran, and ten million other handicaps. My karma happens to be idiotic vanity and a propensity to gamble. Get over it. Everyone has to play the cards they're dealt.

And then it struck me. I suddenly looked at Solitaire a totally different way. It's frustrating as hell to be dealt a bad hand so often, barely break even with a lot of effort and concentration. Wow, the deal was IMPERSONAL, had nothing to do with me, just a random shuffle of cards that the computer dealt and that anyone else would have equal trouble playing!

Holy smokes. No wonder other people don't risk everything to write a novel. The odds are sky high 33-to-1 against sweeping all 52 cards to the win line. Jeez. I have to talk to my writer pals, to congratulate them individually again for going naked in public (that's what writing a novel is like) no guarantee of winning a nickel of profit and undoubtedly risking something of value, wearing the hairshirt of creative life and dragging a preposterously difficult idea to and from bed involuntarily, daring to envision a complicated finished product that smashes a literary barrier, something that no one else has done before, original work!

My pal Tom Ruppenthal has been a creative ally for nearly 50 years, all the way back to our first 16mm film experiments. Guess what he sent me a couple days ago? A television script, episode #1 for a sitcom that's set 40,000 years ago with a Neanderthal cast that speaks in gibberish.

I have nothing to complain about. Tom's in much bigger trouble creatively, because the script is pretty damn good (albeit unintelligible and kind of icky). Fifty-page TV scripts and series bibles do not fall out of the sky. They take weeks and often months to develop, rough draft, and then polish. Tom is betting his reputation on it. Think about it. He's been wrestling with Neanderthals day and night for weeks, plotting how to do such a thing as a comedy.

Stunned. Absolutely stunned. Another deal of Solitaire cards — Tom's turn to play as carefully and shrewdly as possible with the craziest thing that anyone has ever attempted. Worse: it's interesting and I can make it work if I was directing. A silent movie sitcom with gibberish. Icky but compelling, might be right for Netflix, an English translation closed captioned. LAS Spanish captions for another couple million viewers. German! Japanese! Chinese! — as simple and cheap as translating the captions, and we can tailor the verbal humor for each market!

Creative life is simple. Go naked in public, tell the world This is Me, this is something that I concocted, and I sweat bullets to make it a polished gem, with all the maturity and talent that I could muster. Well done, Tommy.

Neanderthal comedy 40,000 years ago in a cave ... golly!

Reefer madness

Zionist neo-con radio star Hugh Hewitt is convinced that smoking marijuana makes people schizophrenic. (Is that why they oppose wars of choice?) Pot smokers don't earn as much money as brave, clean, and reverent Catholics. (Right. They don't bend over and perform rituals.)

Is it really necessary to relitigate reefer again? It's nice that you have big money and prestige, talking nonstop at lightning speed three hours daily on the radio. It's an awesome talent in a highly competitive racket. I'm convinced that your "Fetching Mrs. Hewitt" is quite a gal, if a smidgeon less fetching than she used to be.

Where we part ways is your bromance with John Boulton and Chuck Todd. You and they were disgusted by Donald Trump until he won the 2016 nomination and beat Hillary. Now you think you're qualified to be umpires, "calling balls and strikes" with perfect objectivity and greater wisdom than Trump. Nothing has changed. Your strike zone agenda is Israel first, last, and always, punctuated by trivia about college sports, pro sports, and advertisers doing God's work, the Salem revenue aspect of which you have to conceal while passionately pitching how important the advertised charity is, according to the continuity script in front of you.

I've listened to you as much as I can stomach from time to time. The only thing to your credit is better coherence than Bill Bennett, who you replaced in morning drive. A pretty low bar, but you keep stumbling over it with moronic crap like Tarzana Joe and compulsive pokes at Steelers fans. You're not a guy that I would deem a serious person, nor much of a showman.

"Morning glory?" — a true believer, Israel uber alles, no different than Mark Levin, another ex-government yes man, oh so proud, like you. Neither of you could win elected office. Learning 'Con Law' can be done via mobile device. Unless you include James Otis, the principles of equity, Causes of Taking Up Arms, and the Legal Tender Cases in your syllabus, the modern liberal dicta masquerading as case law forces impressionable students to swallow poisonous doctrine and say yum, we like arbitrary government, more work for lawyers!

Lay off cheap targets like pot smoking, please. If you want to criticize someone's behavior, blow the lid off gay Hollywood, or all the Goldman alumni in positions of public trust worldwide.

Wait a minute. I'll agree with you. Pot is really bad. Let's pry open pot-smoking Barry Obama's admission records at Columbia, see if he registered as a foreign student. I don't care about Bill Clinton smoking pot. He was too stupid to inhale it, allegedly. Why would he lie? Do you remember the financial crisis of 2008 and "F.O.B." (Friends of Bill) who made serious money in Alt-A and liar loan origination backed by GSEs that Clinton unleashed? Am I imagining it or was Rahm Emmanuel put in charge of Fannie or Freddie in the salad years? Say it ain't so.

Typical pothead memory dysfunction. I'll have to check Wikipedia, a pothead achievement, like Apple was. Oh my God, Hugh, you don't use a godless hippie iPhone, do you? Say it ain't so. Bad enough that Limbaugh does. Oh wait. Rush has considerably better numbers, tells jokes, doesn't run his mouth as rapidly as possible. Probably stoned. I wouldn't put it past him.

Cheer up, dude. Console yourself with the knowledge that you're smarter than Mike Gallagher, and smarmy Medved got canned. Makes me smile that he's gone. Let's celebrate by playing Jaggar's "Under My Thumb." Strut, Hugh, strut! -- if you can find the backbeat.

An unfunny world

"It's a funny old world," W.C. Fields muttered with a cynical drawl, "You're lucky if you get out of it alive."

Well, yes. Especially if you oppose the mob. "The course of each great cultural step forward runs like this: a genius makes a great discovery; he is fought, opposed, persecuted, ridiculed, denounced in every way possible; he is made a martyr. He has to pay for his discovery and for his greatness, pay in suffering, poverty, obscurity, insults, and sometimes in actual arrest, jail, and death." (Ayn Rand)

I don't want to die in poverty or prison, then be rediscovered and celebrated someday "in a better world," as Brant Gaede suggested. Better worlds do not arise spontaneously, and Rand was right, it amounts to expropriation and larceny if I don't benefit while I'm alive to enjoy some sliver of reward. Tempts me to destroy everything that I wrote. Screw the future.

C-c-c-cold

Winter all of a sudden, freezing at night, up every couple hours to add wood to the stove, a nice new airtight that does an excellent job of heating the whole house, a function of smart architecture, foam insulation and earth berms. I pity folks nearby who have old leaky wood houses — or a cold tin barn like my writing office at the bottom of a frosty hollow.

I cannot imagine what it's like in Kathmandu or Fairbanks, the two frozen outposts where my work was recognized enthusiastically. It must be subzero in Alaska and Nepal, buried under sparkling snow, no different than Sibera. Huh. Maybe I should ask somebody to translate my novels and nonfiction into Russian, to advance my fame in another icy wilderness.

I grew up in Wisconsin and hated winter, never liked it. I thought of my boyhood when a cold front swept down from Canada. I was nine years old in the basement of a snowbound frame house, shoveled coal in a hopper, then pulled stony clinkers out of the furnace, hard work for a skinny kid. Our basement coal bin was as big as a bedroom, black and cold, lit with a single bulb that had a pull chain. Primitive stuff, but it kept us warm in Fox Valley winter.

Less certain whether I can keep warm in the tin barn this winter. I worry about using propane to fire the barbeque grill parked in my writing office. Makes good heat, but my little bottle of fuel goes fast, $14 to refill it, if I get lucky and catch a ride to the general store. In summer, it's pleasant walking a half mile to the general store for food and cigarettes. We had an unusually warm October and November — then, suddenly, wham, winter, bundled up with a wool hat and ski jacket, ski gloves that I have to shed if I want to do something on the keyboard. I can't seem to stop writing, as if my final days might be near and I can't waste a single hour, writing with frozen fingers and a runny nose. I splurged and bought a box of tissues. Excuse me while I blow my nose. Do Siberians have Kleenex?

Makes sense that my work is read in frozen wastelands, instead of balmy Hollywood. People in cold climates read books, stay near the fire, can't get a decent TV signal with snow draped on transmitter towers, satellite dishes filled with thick ice. Now that I think about it, Nepal and Siberia probably don't have cable or multiplayer internet games, that's why they read. I never saw anyone crack a book in Costa Rica, far too nice on hot white sand beaches in winter, idyllic warmth that anyone with sense should enjoy, instead of living in a walk-in freezer, praying for more propane and warming up by splitting more firewood, more kindling.

I like writing, however uncomfortable it is to clench and shake my cold hands and feet. Maybe I should wear double socks, double T-shirts under the Italian sweater that I haven't washed in several years, scared to ruin it with soap. Like most other worries, it's irrational. Sweaters are designed to be washed, no different than cotton shirts and slacks. What's kept me from doing it in winter is simple. The sweater keeps my core warm, can't part with it for an hour to let it drip dry next to the wood stove. I certainly wish that I had extra long johns. Pretty cold waiting for them to wash and tumble in a dryer, uncertain if they'll last another winter.

I shouldn't complain. Los Angeles is fighting wildfires deliberately set to punish the wealthy, relative humidity in single digits and plenty of brush to burn Bel Air, Ventura, San Diego and Santa Barbara to the ground, sunny places where people never read books, have a thousand channels of widescreen amusement, no intellectual focus or imagination required.

How the hell can gangbangers keep killing each other in drive-by shootings on icy, windswept Chicago streets? Winter is the time to stay indoors and read. Oh, wait. They can't read.

Secret agents

I'm a civilian, too old to be anything else. Most of my friends are civilians. If I need help, I can summon civilian cops and doctors. In my travels around the world, I flew on civilian aircraft, rode in civilian vehicles and trains, encountered thousands of civilians on streets and in hotels and restaurants. I consulted civilian lawyers, signed civilian rental agreements and employment contracts, bought stuff in civilian shops, directed civilian film crews, sat in civilian offices and studios.

Americans, Australians, and Europeans have civilian governments constrained by public policy and legal processes that reflect civilian opinions and needs. Whether Britain is a civil society is debatable. Like China and Russia, they have a sovereign "civil service" that exists independently of the civilians they rule. Elsewhere, government is a tyranny, especially in black Africa, a bright line of division between power and powerlessness, no civilians as such, only masters and serfs.

I brought up this subject to talk about something else. Whether civilian life is mostly free or frustrated by government, there is an entirely separate community (for lack of a better term) worlds apart from civilians and bureaucrats. Its most benign regiments are military. I like old soldiers, Marines in particular. I understand them. War is hell. Emotional wounds are deep. Vietnam veterans have horrible stories to tell. I listen to them, treat them as equals in life, because I understand.

It would be nice if the uncivil community was limited to military men, but it's not. There is a subset of warriors who take no prisoners and have no regard for civilians or political life. They operate independently, no different than criminals or beasts of prey. From time to time these ruthless men and women are authorized to kill, deceive, change their identities and disappear, ineligible for military benefits because they aren't military. Whether American, English, Russian, Levantine, French, or Israeli, secret agents are monsters.

I was never comfortable in their company. Human life is unimportant. Murder and deceit is their mission, kill or be killed. Nations do not exist for them. They change sides depending on financial opportunity, a window to crawl through, a deal, a temporary anchor in action. They have lovers, but no friends. Obligation is an alien concept -- something that loyal military men honor proudly. Covert identity is a forged passport, an assumed name, a disguise.

They began life as civilians and most have had military training. At some point they were in secret service authorized by a government agency, but had no support, no legal remit. They were given a task that stripped them of official protection. Entering into the underworld of covert operations is a one way journey, never to return home, no happy retirement. Leaders of U.S. intelligence agencies have been murdered, covert operators routinely captured and tortured and disposed of.

Why do such men (it's mostly men) exist? Because lawful agents, commercial or political or military, are incapable of controlling a cruel, anarchistic world. Secret operators are the heroes and villains who struggle to do what civilians and armies of disciplined military forces cannot do. It is a form of deliberate suicide, a temptation to throw oneself into the fires of hell and smirk at conventional authority.

It's an historic role, and it's contagious, seducing whole societies with the imperative of evil operations in private life. All's fair in love and war, right? Tens of thousands of Mexicans are dead, decapitated, burned alive, because warlords and graft were spawned by governments on both sides of the border. A wall would help, perhaps, but there is no border wall that cannot be penetrated by special operators, whether criminal or formerly "official" gone rogue.

I like being a simple civilian, safe and snug in a community of good neighbors, folks who plow fields and harvest crops, milk cows, work in factories, operate heavy equipment, build homes and highways. I like the orderly civilian realm of banks, grocery stores, auto repair, radio stations and hospitals. Great fun to visit a restaurant, order a meal and pay for it, an implicit contract. Civilian life is cooperative, law abiding and rarely cruel, an unearned gift bequeathed by secret agents whose lives were sacrificed to do hellish brutality, kill or be killed.

Criminal enterprise

Bill suggested that I write a history of Laissez Faire City. I can do it in a single sentence. It was a criminal enterprise. Details would fill a shelf as big as a two-volume O.E.D., defining each aspect and utilizing nearly every word in the English language. With equal mental energy and all of my remaining days, I could fill a library with crimes committed by millions of other people, including the Massachusetts Bay Colony, the Founding Fathers, and every session of Congress since its inception as an institution of political compromise.

The dispossessed native Amerindians were rapacious brutes, perpetually at war with rival tribes and far worse in their treatment of women and children than the bloody Aztecs and Arabs. One cannot point to a single African tribe ancient or modern that has clean hands, or an instance of religion or philosophy that did not punish the weak. You think that libertarians are innocent? Hah. Murray Rothbard was supported by taxation and tax loopholes his entire life. Walter Block laughed that a Ph.D. in economics was a $250,000 annual meal ticket to do little as a tentured party animal, funded by similar political crimes, including intellectual fraud.

I claim innocence in that regard. I was an innovator. I was also ignored and exiled, the strange karma of working outside the iron grip of tradition and scholarship of the Known and Familiar. Those who succeed intellectually, creatively, or economically are slaves to the art of extracting maximum benefit from existing arrangements. I'm typing these words on a laptop made in China, built by indentured servants from a series of stepwise improvements following basic research at Bell Labs, a monopoly, led by an asshole guilty of multiple crimes.

I try to be generous about crime. Life is short. Few of us are born free and independent of life's little boxes. Whatever joy one finds is usually a happy accident, someone to love, far removed from the world, cloistered in a hovel or something less awkward depending on one's continent and era of history. Sexual love has existed for thousands of years, perhaps the only personal value that is discovered and earned, threatened by success and treachery, won and lost, transformed irrevocably by the purpose of sex — children.

You were once a child, the product of sexual love, something that may have been a mistake in judgment, fogged by animal physiology, no different than other species. The bonds and boxes of family or lack thereof shape who we are as people. That Austrian economics is deaf to this principle explains why libertarianism remains an inarticulate craving for high crimes and misdemeanors, baseline treason. Let's compare and contrast a life of duty. My best fiction stars a USMC officer who resigned his commission because he was revulsed by killing, the sole mission of Marines, devil dogs trained to fight as a team, to obey every command unquestioningly and immediately without flinching from peril. Marines are frontline infantrymen tasked to take real estate and hold it by force.

Without such men we would not be having this conversation. In ancient times, Marines were the stiff backbone of maritime empire, stationed shipboard to enforce order and attack on shore, expeditionary forces to win supplies and defeat all opposition. Cannonade (in modern times aerial bombardment) cannot take, it can only destroy. Marines take territory and resources. Troops organized into an Army are clumsy in operation, fueled by a deluxe supply chain and leisurely well planned deployment. Marines land first, poorly equipped except by their fierce character as fighting men.

I speak of these matters to highlight our collective debt to crime. Whether it's Israel or USA, history is a trail of tears, unending war, political oppression, economic waste and fraudulent claims of wisdom and justice. Through it all, sex and family shaped what men did and why. Their women reared children to enter into battle with each other and for or against the men in power. Transition to a modestly peaceful postwar civil society in the late 20th century is comfortable, but little else has changed. Sex and family still determine our destiny.

The challenge of liberty is to make a choice, to join the Marines or avoid duty. I'm not certain which is more honorable. As a small and sensitive man, I was ill suited to fighting. I avoided fights as a child, as a young man, and later in life as a filmmaker. Had I been more aggressive and ruthless, I could have won a more successful career in Hollywood, I'm certain of it, and I could recite a string of incidents in which I was self-defeated by cowardice. I turned down an opportunity to make a slasher movie, fully funded and easily done. I abhor violence.

That does not make me an antiwar libertarian. The fact of the matter is that my survival and happiness depend on U.S. Marines and their overlords, who manufacture government and capital goods. Using the platform of luxury that we all share in the modern world, I'm writing an article on the topic of crime. It was not a crime to fight the American Revolutionary War of Independence, nor any of the global conflicts that predated my life. What happened in Vietnam and more recently Iraq was tragedy, rather than sudden perversion of American power. Nothing surpassed the perversion of American life by slavery and the Civil War. There is endless suffering to come, a nation divided by DNA. The melting pot theory is rhetorical and theoretical.

It's not my purpose to complain. The goal of my work has been to advance a few ideas that could influence history, principally a new constitutional framework for the practice of law and the profession of justice. It was a job that I did not volunteer to undertake. I was forced to swear it as a solemn purpose, after spending two years in Federal prison and observing many cases among the men who were likewise deemed felons. I did time with Gordon Liddy. I bunked with murderers, bank robbers, drug dealers, and white collar criminals. Every one of them had families and children, enjoyed music, wanted freedom and prosperity. As a jailhouse lawyer, I freed three of them, however the challenge of discerning apolitical constitutional law as it might and ought to be was a daunting task.

It only took 25 years to make good on that mission, to redefine justice and to frame an organic document constituting laissez faire law.

The achievement was a great burden of duty that finally ended, thank goodness. It was done at a time when Laissez Faire City was in need of due process of law. Had it been ratified as a constitutional legal regime, it could have saved Laissez Faire City from implosion. No free society can survive without the rule of law.

We should be careful when using that phrase, the rule of law. It has nothing to do with the whims of a legislature or tyrant. I will quote an opinion of counsel I filed with the leadership of Laissez Faire City in January 2000, predating the Freeman's Constitution of August 2001, which elaborated this simple idea:

"In a laissez faire community of any kind, physical or digital, the rule of law arises from and requires all of the following: a constitutional right to practice legal representation on behalf of others; the right of practicing lawyers to associate for the purpose of selecting judges who, on appointment to the bench, are barred from private legal practice; and the right of any person or organized group to obey and execute lawful orders that may be issued from time to time by the courts so created. The jursidiction of laissez faire constitutional law and the courts which duly interpret and uphold such principles exists globally and perpetually as a matter of right. Laissez faire constitutional law flows from a single proposition, which is that no one may legally judge his own cause of action or act to penalize another without fair public trial and impartial due process of law. Laissez faire law is discovered and demonstrated in the process of litigation and trial. It cannot be legislated, codified, or imposed by a 'lawgiver'."

Whether that makes sense to you or not is unimportant. What I wish to impart is extremely simple. Laissez faire justice set forth in The Freeman's Constitution was an act of treason, no different than the Declaration of Independence in 1776. The quarto volume of my book Laissez Faire Law paid tribute to our gallant forefathers by choosing the Amazon retail price of $17.76

Croissants

For two years, my third wife and I lived on a ranch in Northern California, caretakers to feed the horses, sheep, llamas, and chickens. I fought a war against blue jays, dozens of them that raided the hen house daily. I built 2x6 fences, repaired outbuildings, painted the farmhouse, split wood for the winter, and helped to fight a forest fire. I listened to BBC World Service on a shortwave radio and wrote a great deal, made videos and pitched movie projects, went to Los Angeles a couple times to attend a Hollywood funeral and a Malibu wedding.

However, the single most memorable aspect of life on the ranch was croissants. I think of it frequently, decades later, thought of it again last night. She taught me how to make bread dough in a bowl, one of the most difficult chores imaginable. Bread dough starts easily, water and flour, then more flour and more flour, until it's almost impossible to move with a spoon. "Women's work!" I quipped in exasperation, because it was tiring and difficult. Following directions by an amused wife, I grabbed the damn blob and began to fold it and knead it, roll more flour into it, beat the shit out of it until it was supple, stretchy, and ready for the oven. Homemade bread is wonderful, well worth the effort.

It became an object lesson in hubris. She sliced the bread dough into thin strips and folded them into beautifully shaped coissants, which sounded swell. We had enough pans, but not enough room in our pokey propane oven. I scoffed. "Put that last pan on the bottom of the oven," I advised. Oh, no, we never do that, she explained, and I stupidly insisted that heat was the same everywhere in an oven. Men think they know things. She reluctantly obeyed. Sure enough, the floor of the oven turned that last pan of croissants into black ashes.

Is there anything else to say? Perhaps. A more thoughtful person, a female (say, for instance, novelist Cass McMain) is worth hearing and heeding. Numerous friends have attempted from time to time to offer good counsel. No joke, I mean it. I have been profoundly stubborn, took ridiculous chances, burned bridges, wasted most of my life doing the wrong thing.

Now in my late 60s, penniless, credit kaput, and no longer cute enough to win an unearned ribbon of luxury, I begin each day looking at trio of book covers that I created, ugly ducklings on my Windows desktop background, pasted there to confront reality when I open my laptop each morning. I spent two years full time writing an unwanted, politically insensitive saga. Having absorbed the lesson of croissants, I made the hero a little stupid, his female partner a genius. With greater insight, I should have written nothing at all and used those two years to make money at a regular job, instead of shattering personal finances and self-esteem. I sold my car to finish the third novel, reduced to the dreary humiliation of walking on dirt roads to the general store for bread and lunch meat, a bag of dog treats for an old blind shihtzu.

It's a well known fact that self-publishing is death, no different than ashes on the bottom of an oven. Agents and book publishers won't touch a self-published author, and I have had no success on Kindle or IngramSpark or Createspace or Lulu. Tens of thousands of dollars down the drain, no sales revenue, a couple books purchased by friends, an act of benevolence.

Soon it will be winter, too cold to huddle in the tin barn and write. Whether I like it or not, it makes sense to turn off the power, save $30 a month, lock the door and walk away from my writing office and burbling coffee pot. It won't be the first time that I failed in a creative venture. That's actually a cheery thought in a perverse sense — previous endeavors burned millions of dollars of other people's money. No joke. That's what filmmakers do. Everybody expects the show to succeed, a profitable gamble. Mine flopped every fucking time, no one else to blame but myself. Directors come in all sizes and dispositions. I was a tyrant auteur with final cut.

Whether it's writing a novel or directing a movie, it's all the same thing — authorship, a solo flight of daring. I don't regret my life. Swans do not regret being swans. I miss the companionship and comfort of intimacy, but romantic love properly belongs to the young, and I'm no longer young. I'm not even certain that I regret smoking 400,000 cigarettes. We're not talking about practical life or good counsel, neither of which deflect an artist. A different life would have won comfortable retirement and the deep joy of grandparenthood. I have two grandchildren I never visit, who know nothing about me. It hurts, but the price of being an artist includes sacrificing life's simple joys. One's life is fuel for the flames on a page or a television screen. I had a shot at the big screen, muffed it, and suffered grievously for it. No one stopped me from taking my turn on the high wire, working without a net. I crashed to the hard turf of despair, took years to heal, my reputation and career opportunities destroyed.

That's what happened with Chris and Peachy, a blaze of courage that turned to ashes. I look at my book covers and, when a few days or weeks elapse, I re-read my work and marvel at each word, every page. I know for a fact that I will never write so well again, perhaps never write another word of fiction. That's the price of art. Spend every last sous and honor it. No one cares to read what I wrote. Is it LGBT? — emphatically not. Chick lit? Cozy mystery? — nope. Hardboiled ghetto gangstas and drug addled hos? — yeah, right.

Chris and Peachy are privileged white people, Ivy League, wealthy and happy and clean, connected to powerful men in Deep State covert operations, with Marine Corps valor, absolute independence, and sex scenes that will make you blush.

Ooops.

Fitzgerald

I like writing in the morning, fresh and rested. No subject seems intractable. For instance, late last night Greta urged me to fart on F. Scott Fitzgerald, because he wasted his talent. I mumbled that imagery and turn of phrase inspired me, implying that I was easily led. What I should have said was: Don't trust me with a typewriter — I might say any darn thing! -- with Fitzgerald's understanding and approval. He and I suffer the identical intellectual disease, way too self-absorbed, inebriated most of the time, indifferent to duty.

Compare the sober excellence of a great surgeon, a physicist, an engineer, farmer, or airline pilot. Grandfathers on both sides of my family tree were brilliant businessmen, brought to life enormous dedication and trustworthiness, built factories and raised big families, made their communities stronger. Fitzgerald scoffed at them, so did I. There is a smugness about such men, a blockheadedness in the conviction that life is mapped and wrangled with an accounting statement, a flight plan, a bible of good practice — all of which is perfectly good and wise and necessary unless you're a creative sod. It happens from time to time, despite the upright example of sniffy Methodists and benevolent Freemasons who expect you to agree. Libertines are the loose screws that fell through a crack in the shop floor. I think that's how I parted company with good government, an unintended and exasperating accident of orderly Midwestern mass production.

Fitzgerald was an infinitely better writer, which I acknowledge freely. He pilloried Hollywood a hell of lot better than I have. My thing is sex, notably absent from better literature. It's on my mind again this morning because an admirer mentioned it in a gushing LinkedIn message. I have a handful of admirers, grateful that I explained what to do with women. In the All-Purpose Guide, I counseled gentlemen to seek an intelligent equal, dance with her, get the music and lighting right in the living room.

Sigh. Like Scott Fitzgerald, my gifts were exhausted decades ago. In an egotistical interview documentary, I said mentors bestow one boon per student. Everything else is footnotes and fuzzy authorities that one regrets reading. Roscoe Pound was an exception, a singular voice among millions of erudite punks like Barack Obama. Lawyer jokes are richly deserved, although I was luckier than most men, had good attorneys to help get things done. The point is that Roscoe Pound had a special gift in legal theory, clear and concise. I did the same thing with sex. Fitzgerald did it with worthless heirs.

You'd think that they should logically intersect, sex and playboys, but they don't. Worthless heirs have stupid notions and stupid preferences. One thinks of boors, too many to mention, daily headlines, no different than Fitzgerald's millieu in the Jazz Age. The yellow press is a lot louder nowadays, but nothing has fundamentally changed. Rich boys are embarrassing, not the least bit interested in seducing an equal. In Fitzgerald's masterpiece *Tender Is The Night*, a reasonably good fellow, a middle class guy with a good brain, is slowly and surely destroyed by the seduction of wealth. In the end, every franc is taken from him by a mercenary.

Simple stories. Life is a one way street. In 'The Four Punches' and 'Dalrymple Goes Wrong,' Fitzgerald says we get few clues, and the ones we discover take most of the fun out of living. He had the gift of tragedy. 'May Day' should be required reading in every high school.

Oh, how easy it was for me to wail and keen, a lost lamb among wolves. That's not tragedy, it's pathos! I think I outgrew it after an extended adolescence, some forty or fifty years of petulance. My recent work is a blend of Balzac and RLS, the preposterous business of manly adventure with overheated romance, to put it politely. No wonder I have fewer friends. I kept at it because Fitzgerald was a pioneer who made me a grateful chump, in love with each moment of literary life, knowing the price it exacted.

Let's conclude with a good joke. An elderly neighbor lady has been exceptionally kind to me, fed me and kept me stoned, so I could continue as a novelist. She read the first draft of my Portrait of Valor, and in reaction she observed: "You've had sex before."

Greed

Why do I get stuck explaining things? Jeez.

Michael Medved bungled again, couldn't explain capitalism. Pay attention, dipshit. Investors have to climb a wall of worry. Competition, hidden defects in the enterprise or management thereof, cost of money, foreign exchange rates, and two million other factors like deliberate market rigging by colocated robots and short sellers could wipe out investor gains in a blink. That's why professional investors strangle positions with puts, calls, and stop orders.

Meanwhile, corporations are NOT eager to take on more debt, unless their market share is hopeless (like Sears). Bankruptcy and liquidation (Borders, Toys R Us) is better than sudden mark-down of shale gas asset value (Chesapeake). Investors in Venezuela were totally screwed. If a borrower can't pay and never made a profit, high yield lenders face financial disaster (Uber, Tesla). That's why retail investors prefer mutual funds and pension funds that spread bets across several asset classes: blue chip dividends, bonds, real estate, Treasurys, gold, and high P/E multiple FANG stocks (Facebook, Apple, Netflix, Google).

Profitable companies expand and launch new products with retained earnings. R&D is a pre-tax deduction. They pay top wages to attract the best employees and put considerable effort into world class organizational development (Boeing, IBM).

"Greed" drives half of it. If they can't make a profit, publicly traded companies lose market value, pay higher interest rates, shrink and die (AT&T taken over by Southwest Bell for $1 and assumption of AT&T's debt, Enron liquidated without paying pensions). "Fear" is an equally harsh factor. Many companies are vulnerable to Chinese competitors and trade tariffs.

Households are no different. "Greed" encourages people to go to college, to butter up family and classmates. Fear makes them stick at a job they despise while they look for something better, and in the meantime smile at the boss, pretend to be a loyal servant. The ultimate greed is liberty, greatest fear a Blue Wave to impose higher taxes and job-killing regulation.

Pretty simple stuff. Liberty promotes greed and squashes risk. Capitalism is profits, savings, and retained earnings, invested in new products, new hiring, better wages, business expansion, and "creative destruction" of inefficient and unneeded stuff (horse-drawn plows, steam locomotives, whale oil, telegraphy).

If you want to punish greed, engine of a wealthier society, enact laws abolishing civil liberty and private property, multiplying fear and want (Venezeula, North Korea).

I could have been someone

I know I'm quite stupid, but it could have been different. I clocked 145 IQ as a kid. Probably about 80 now, a big palette of useless skills. Funny thing about intelligence testing, doesn't measure math aptitude or the ability to memorize big stacks of facts. I excelled at logic.

So, what could a bright dumbshit have done in life? — anything involving physical reality, nuts and bolts, mechanical design, optics, machining, soldering, welding, wiring, assembly, troubleshooting and testing — all of which I did as a kid and later in life. I had talent as an architect, graphic artist, furniture designer, filmmaker, audio tech, lighting tech. I covered thousands of pages in complicated diagrams, built prototypes and systems.

Ooo, bad news. Destined to be a second or third banana. The top earners are businessmen and bankers, number guys who invent nothing and shave pennies, roll them into dollars. Doctors and lawyers have minds like computers, stuffed with detailed info and generally accepted best practice. I didn't have the attention span of a gnat, unless I was designing something original.

Nor did I have the gift of gab, the hallmark of a salesman. I was a terrible presenter, tongue tied and shy, never at ease unless I was working alone and imagining an unique solution. Always got a kick out of designing speaker systems, brilliant highs and thundering bass, using cheap components and series-parallel power division. Simple stuff. Writing is like that. Words are cheap, but they can be combined in original ways with acoustic power. I don't write anything with scholarly or literary elegance. Show me the main panel and stand back, you might need a fire extinguisher.

Immoral

While the rest of the country is goo-goo about Fred Rogers and throwing furniture at Donald Trump, I've been doing something less infantile. I finished a novel that required 1000 hours and $1000 to write. Intellectual investments aren't cheap. During the past three years, I've done that repeatedly, burned every cell of psychic power and every dollar at my disposal to create a literary legacy. Some of the money was mine, some of it was ponied up by friends and credit cards. The total could be measured in cans of coffee, cartons of cigarettes, ounces of pot, hundreds of thousands of words, or dozens of times that I've been dissed and cursed by my wife and daughter. You get what you pay for in life. I threw myself in the furnace of creative work.

Along the way, from time to time, I scratched on the walls like a prisoner. My writing office has a wall of paneling that I installed to seal up bare framing. Three years ago, the new wall was covered with an outline for Mars. Then a list of characters for A Portrait of Valor. About a year ago, I pasted duct tape to spell out a math equation, two feet tall, $2 + 1 = 0$. Two years of writing plus one year to build a house had won me nothing. Six months ago, I summed up my career as a storyteller, over 20 years of writing. I believe it to be an accurate self assessment, written in grease pencil on the wall, my Sharpie dry, no car or cash to buy another:

1. Retired

2. Exiled

3. Untalented

4. Stupid

5. Immoral

The first four items are excusable. I'm not the only snowflake who made an idiotic decision, believing wrongly that writing books was a good idea. Goodreads has 50,000 equally dumb self-published authors. As an experiment in promotion, I joined a Goodreads review group, reciprocal praise for featherweight crap. I got thrown out and banished because I refused to read and review a randomly assigned novel that was written by an illiterate dolt. Sometimes I think that writing should be a licensed profession.

Perhaps it is. I pitched dozens of agents and publishers, rejected every time. That's one of the reasons why I'm self-published, unread, ignored. Far more important to me personally, my work is archived in digital files at Lulu and Amazon. My laptop has screen cancer, and I didn't trust my heirs to perceive any value in my immoral output.

That's what distinguishes Wolf DeVoon from the other fifty thousand nitwits. The stories I write are immoral. My people are loose cannons, indifferent to the general welfare. They fall in love and fuck like minks, graphically told. They are straight white rich people, armed and dangerous, ready to kill or be killed. How immoral or politically incorrect can one be?

In this, I had little choice. The literature I admired was straight white: Ayn Rand, Robert Louis Stevenson, Raymond Chandler, Dashiell Hammett, F. Scott Fitzgerald, Eugene Rhodes, C.S. Forester. All of their heroes were armed and dangerous.

I look at the modern world and feel sorry for my contemporaries. Their heroes are fags and harpies. Guns are too dangerous to touch, votes sacrosanct. I have friends who are LEOs and Federal agents, hamstrung by cowards, politicians, and community organizers, none of whom has to face life on life's terms, alone in the dead of night, kill or be killed. I like due process as well as the next fellow, but law courts move like molasses, months or years after someone fought for liberty and justice, shot a dangerous thug in the line of duty.

I studied and admired the Sons of Liberty, the Committee of Safety, and Continental Congress. Our nation was founded by straight white people, defended throughout two centuries of American history by men who put their lives on the line. What gays have contributed is obscene and impotent, a conspiracy of postal clerks and twinks. If I'm the last American novelist who celebrates manhood, fine. I'll take opprobrium, poverty, and humiliation gladly.

40% of the Los Angeles city bureaucracy is black — and you wonder why it's inept and corrupt? Detroit, Chicago, and Baltimore were destroyed by black voters and black city councils. That welfare recipients can vote is insane, generation after generation who are housed and fed by avowed communists and "public service" looters masquerading as educators. You're a dope, whitey, hunted like prey by street gangs and tax collectors. Go ahead, vote for more sanctuary cities and open borders. You deserve nothing better than MS-13 and Mexican cartels.

It makes me laugh and smile, that Donald Trump is rich, white, and fabulously successful as a straight guy who loves beautiful women, married to elegant Melania. Up yours, Barack and Michelle, Bill and Hillary, last gasp of a corrupt "ethical" superstructure that no one needed, an object lesson in civics. The press can wring their hands and wail, but the jig is up. American civilization is white, not colorblind or stupid. Freedom means freedom from government, lower taxes, strong borders, and civilian law enforcement, three quarters of it provided by private guards and the Second Amendment, an American common law right to defend ourselves.

It's the theme of my next project, food and coffee and health permitting.

Intensely proud

I opened Finding Flopsie tonight, skipped past the soap opera set-up and went straight to Chris on his own, losing his teaching job, his office, his p.i. license, and his pride, all in one afternoon. Absolutely terrific -- and then the story takes off on urgent business, active and grim, Chris Cable at his best, age 64. Whether I got Peachy's story right is debatable, but it simply had to be that way, role reversal with her evil sister, a tortured animal.

Not much to say about Partners, my masterwork.

I cleaned up Mars Shall Thunder for the anthology Eight Ruthless Novels, happy with it and proud of it, my first full-length novel. The Good Walk Alone was a rolicking comedy, free as a lark, fun to write, drove me crazy writing a serial to weekly deadline. DiMarco remains my favorite character of all, a tough female homicide cop, age 38. I don't know quite what to say about First Feature. Personal stories are holy, if anything pertaining to show business is.

The Case Files trilogy (Valor, Tar Pit, and Charity) are what they had to be, a modern Nick and Nora, to honor Dashiell Hammett's final novel The Thin Man, a burlesque that broke the noir genre, gave us penthouse cocktail parties and sexy women as a backdrop to murder. Chris and Peachy are a little different, equals in life, an unbeatable team. A Portrait of Valor tests them to the limit of human daring and spiritual endurance at the peak of their vitality, 30-something, deeply in love for the first time, perfectly matched in marriage. In many ways Valor is my favorite story. Boy meets girl and they go to heaven and hell to earn each other. Being childless opens the door to an important truth, the wider moral horizons of Charity. In our calm, clever 50s, new life happens if we embrace it.

I suppose it's true that all of my stories are aspects of my personal life, things that happened to me, one way or another, amplified a notch or two. I wrote about people and places I knew well enough to speak confidently. I had a life full of adventure. A little sad that it's over, but that's part of life, too. No one likes to talk about the end, and it would be wrong to paint the final chapter of any fictional character's slow demise. Bad enough that I have to do it.

Nice to leave a literary legacy, the splendor of young adulthood and active middle age, great eagerness to thrive, a whole world to gamble and win -- or to lose, in the tragedy of Partners, a story that I did not expect to create. Partners was costly, in time and talent and weight of burden, everything I had to give and endure, the capstone of my career. I know it for a fact, I worked 20 years to prepare myself to write Partners. Completely unexpected and worth it.

Truthfully, I don't recommend that anyone else pursue a creative career. The field is occupied by hostile assholes and pusillanimous slime. Indie self-publishing is a fake solution, gateway to obscurity, sandbagged by Amazon and Google if you stand up for straight white wildcats. I cared about my characters and their circumstances, emptied my wallet to let them breathe and stand fully erect, a proud race of titans. "Old fashioned," Cass declared. So be it. We owe our industrial preeminence and military power to such people, men and women who face a world of tawdry evasion, ritual, and inertia, and kick it into the gutter, where it belongs.

A pity that I wasn't born rich, but if I had been there would be no Chris and Peachy, no Janet DiMarco, no Harry Faraday and Laura Oak, no Kyle and Karen, no Freeman's Constitution to honor and defend them. Pretty good bargain. "Those who fight for the future live in it today," Ayn Rand said. True or false, I'm satisfied that I did everything I could to advance the idea of defacto liberty. Whether sterling hero or hardened criminal, nothing displaces human potential, personal choice, stern perception of values, to live free or to die a coward's dull, anonymous, meaningless end.

The gift of life is not to be thrown away cheaply.

Jeez

What is it with conservative talk radio hosts? -- such knuckleheads that they feel compelled to use a conjunction after the word freedom when they say liberty immediately after it, as if "freedom and liberty" were two separate constitutional objects, which neither of them was. The U.S. Constitution was a charter of power, and not a word of it was written by Alexander Hamilton, dipshits. He proposed monarchy and won little support, so he left the convention after a single week of attendance. The other delegates from New York said that they had no authority to discuss a national government, only to perhaps consider amendments to the Articles of Confederation, so *they* quit the secret Philadelphia assembly, too.

Where did you get the idea that the Constitution was an "inspired" work of legal or political thinking? It was the result of an endless, shameless, mean-spirited, selfish division among Large States and Small States and Free States and Slave States who fought each other for two months, refusing to agree on anything, except a monstrous claptrap that no one wanted to sign until Ben Franklin urged that this ugly baby was their only hope of salvation, a cobbled compromise among 13 bankrupt competitors who were taxing each other as if they were 13 foreign countries. The produce of agricultural New Jersey was compared to a keg tapped at both ends, taxed by Pennsylvania and New York. Those few who spoke of equality and liberty were kneecapped. Either slavery remained legal, or there would be no constitution of any kind. We have a Senate because Slave States and Small States demanded it, refusing to yield to democracy or a republic based on population. The Massachusetts crew were corrupt politicians, angling for power. Elbridge Gerry was the father of *"gerry-mandering,"* argued that state legislators had to retain the privilege of feathering their own nests. Rhode Island delegates were imbeciles, determined to block passage of anything. Counting slaves as 3/5 of a person for the purpose of apportioning representation in Congress was pure payola to entice the Slave States to ratify, doubling the number of seats they would hold in the lower house, a permanent lock on Federal legislation. Ending the importation of slaves was fine. They were breeding them like rabbits, didn't need to import any more, provided that the Crown Lands were stripped from Pennsylvania, who claimed the frontier Ohio Valley. Any new frontier states would be created in pairs, a new slave state for each free one.

Want to know the truth? -- the damn Constitution was a recipe for Civil War — all the anonymous hoopla by Madison, Hamilton, and Jay notwithstanding. The Anti-Federalists in Massachusetts and New York made equally good arguments, and Patrick Henry of Virginia was foursquare against ratification. No one expected the new Constitution to survive more than a few decades.

Don't even get me started on the Bill of Rights, which inverted the notion of enumerated, specific powers, opening the way to Hamilton's doctrine of implied powers and a measly rump of "preferred freedoms" that gave FDR a wink and a nod to regulate every aspect of commerce and use of private property. The only rights remaining are affirmative action in hiring and college admissions, NFL tantrums, throwing rocks at cops, ridiculing President Trump, humiliating Kavanaugh, and gay love as a sacrosanct choice.

Take a look at your wallet, chump. See what is says on your one dollar bill that used to be worth ten times more in purchasing power? It says Federal Reserve Note, an IOU with nada backing it. There's your "originalist" freedom and liberty, an explicit Article I power to coin money and determine the value thereof, no different than the power to levy trade tariffs, the Federal government's sole source of revenue at its inception and specific cause of the Civil War, wiping out five years of national income and 600,000 true believers in justice.

Mark Levin a constitutional scholar? Hahahahahaha.

Exxon's $4 billion offer rejected

This was my debut Alrroya newspaper column published in 2010. That I subsequently wrote and produced an oil industry luncheon video introducing George W. Bush as a "great American leader" goes to show how cheaply a writer can be bought. It took a long time to find photos of W. where he didn't look like a stupid deer caught in the headlights.

In October 2009, I noted ExxonMobil's offer to buy the privately-held Kosmos Energy 24% interest in Ghana's Jubilee oil field. Based on Tullow maps and well data, I deduced that Exxon was using a medium term $100 barrel price model to determine how much to bid for the Kosmos stake. No surprise, it matched forecasts by T. Boone Pickens, Goldman Sachs, and former CIBC World Markets chief economist Jeff Rubin.

Kosmos promptly accepted the Exxon bid, a straightforward move to monetize their Jubilee asset. They were out of pocket less than $1 billion funded by Warburg Pincus and Blackstone Capital Partners. Exxon's $4 billion offer would give them a $3 billion profit and zero their risk of development and doing business in Ghana. Kosmos had previously reduced their risk by farming out stakes to Anadarko and Tullow, who did the actual work of drilling and discovery. Clever little Dallas-based Kosmos achieved what all E&P "minnows" hope to do — get a license, bring in experienced operators, flip it to a fat supermajor. Except the wheels fell off and Exxon's offer died.

Who, why, and what killed the acquisition is a convoluted story. It starts at a racetrack in Dallas involving Texas politicians, a Federal class-action settlement, and a head fake that propelled attorney James C. Musselman to VIP status at a White House state dinner for Ghana's

President John Agyekum Kufour.

Musselman got his start in the oil business as an investor in Triton Energy. He became its CEO in 1998 when Tom Hicks, owner of the Texas Rangers baseball team and chairman of private-equity firm Hicks Muse Tate & Furst, bought a big speculative stake in troubled Triton.

Musselman's job was to pump up reserves and sell the company, which he successfully did in 2001, after reporting an operating loss of $383 million. Hess paid a 50% premium to Triton shareholders, to acquire the Ceiba oil field in Equatorial Guinea. Musselman and his team were deemed geniuses, and they briefly worked for Hess, until Hess had to declare a $530 million impairment charge and write down 70% of the Triton reserves they paid $3 billion to own.

But that's not how it played in Ghana, nor in Dallas where Musselman and his ex-Triton team founded a new company, Kosmos Energy, in 2003. They were touted as West Africa experts with a new project negotiated by Craig S. Glick, who left Hunt Oil with insider knowledge of the West Cape Three Points block in Ghana. Hunt had acquired 2D seismic data totaling 2,225 km and 264 square kilometers of 3D. They drilled and logged two deepwater wells. Those wells were immediately east of the future Jubilee discovery. When Hunt Oil quit Ghana in 2001, the story gets a little bizarre, clogged in multiple layers of state secrets.

Before he became President of the United States, Gov. George W. Bush was co-owner of the Texas Rangers, which he sold to Hicks. After he left the White House, Bush bought a house in the exclusive Preston Hollow neighborhood of Dallas, down the street from Musselman's $6 million mansion. It seems likely that they knew each other in 2003, when Bush met Ghanaian President John Agyekum Kufour in Dakar and urged him to do business with US backing.

Two of Kufour's trusted associates laid the groundwork for a deal with Kosmos. Dr. Kwame Barwuah Edusei, a medical doctor practicing in Washington DC, and George Owusu, a self-styled Ghanaian oil broker living in Houston, formed a company called E-O, rather hilariously registered at a chicken farm near Accra.

Kosmos and E-O entered into a written agreement signed by Edusei for E-O and Glick for Kosmos, covering future exploration and production: Kosmos 86.5%, Ghana National Petroleum Company 10%, E-O 3.5%. The agreement stated that Kosmos would carry E-O and additionally pay them $250,000 upfront. Kufour appointed Edusei his ambassador to Switzerland in August 2004 (to open a numbered account?) and later appointed him Ghana's ambassador to the White House. Owusu became Kosmos Energy's Ghana manager with salary, perks and other graft that may have totaled $2 million before he ran afoul of anti-corruption due diligence by Anadarko.

President Kufour, after serving two four-year terms, had to step down in 2009. He and his cronies did everything possible to grease the wheels for Kosmos, Anadarko, and Tullow — signing off on low royalties, 100% off-loading for export, and token involvement of GNPC. President George W. Bush and First Lady Laura Bush made a 3-day goodwill visit to Ghana in February 2008, meeting all 30 tribal chiefs, promising US development aid, and stumping for Kufour's New Patriotic Party, hoping to upstage and deflate perennial opposition presidential candidate John Atta Mills. In September 2008 there was a gala White House state dinner to honor President Kufour and Kosmos boss Jim Musselman. In Ghana, NPP newspapers and radio stations celebrated fabulous new oil wealth, thanks to Kufour and Kosmos.

All for naught. Social democrat and former national tax commissioner John Atta Mills was elected president of Ghana by a razor-thin majority, after an odd ballot re-run in a remote rural constituency. His first act in office was to appoint a special adviser on energy policy, Tsatsu Tsikata, long-serving patriarch of GNPC who was put in prison and tried for "causing financial loss to the state" when Kufour came to power in 2000. His trial lasted eight years and Tsikata was pronounced guilty, then pardoned when Mills won the 2009 presidential runoff.

Tsikata flew to Houston and visited Anadarko to pick up their Corrupt Foreign Practices file on E-O and Kosmos Ghana. Then he flew to New York and retained Morgan Stanley as financial advisers. Next on the agenda was a $10 billion line of credit from China. Owusu's and E-O's assets were seized. Kosmos was put under investigation.

In 2010, Tsikata flew to China six times, negotiating with CNOOC.

When Kosmos filed a request to sell its interest in Jubilee to Exxon, the government's reaction was comical. In due course, the Energy Ministry said, they would "vet" Exxon and consider their suitability to partner a Ghanaian oil company. They intended to produce Jubilee gas first, because the country needed more electricity generation, and it would hire world class government engineering experts from Trinidad and Tobago. The $4 billion Exxon deal was imaginary and illegal.

The only buyer Kosmos could talk to was Tsatsu Tsikata.

Loner

I monitor conservative talk radio, not because I enjoy it, but because it provides a series of social snapshots. In addition to being pro radio personalities who read advertising copy with perfect enthusiasm, most of them are Jews, a couple evangelicals, all of them 100% patriotic. They loved Ted Cruz and mocked Trump, but reluctantly supported Trump in the general election because they hated Hillary. Conservatives are pragmatic, go along to get along, get richer and more powerful. The worst of the pragmatists is Dennis Prager.

Today, Prager attributed mass murder to "loners" — fatherless atheists who gamble, skate on the wrong side of the Ten Commandments, have no conscience or remorse. I took it at face value and saw myself so described. (I wasn't fatherless; he was an insurance agent.)

Before I discuss it further, please keep in mind that killing is not done exclusively by loners with absent earthly or heavenly fathers. Entire nations led by charismatic fathers killed tens of millions. Groups and gangs are more dangerous than isolated lone wolves. That said, it is true that the tragedy of American urban violence and crime consists primarily of angry lone wolves acting in combination with and/or competition with other lone wolves.

I spent time in prison and met quite a few of these men. They were suspicious and opportunistic, quiet about their history on earth. I'm slightly different in that respect. It has been my habit to talk, reflect, discuss ideas. Perhaps that explains why I sell so few books. No one cares to contemplate what a loner thinks. At best, it's always dark and disturbing.

-- or is it? -- compared to socially accepted product like horror movies? More than a few serial killers were warped by first person shooter video games. Why such stuff exists is pragmatic, big money for Jewish producers and distributors of blood-soaked amusements. I can't watch it. I can't even contemplate the horrible, unless I'm trying to conceive a fictional villain, someone for a hero to fight and defeat. The hero is a far better man than I am, but not so very different, either. Heroes are loners by definition, independent of the approval of others.

It's easy to like policemen and firemen, doctors and lawyers, engineers and heavy equipment operators, auto mechanics who fight with rusted bolts. From time to time I do some of that, show a dab of physical courage, tackle projects involving practical thought and danger, swing heavy tools, balance on ladders and whatnot. If I had to, I could probably shoot to kill, if my wife or daughter were threatened, no different than a cop. Years ago, I fought a forest fire, a so-called "first responder" joined by other neighbors armed with hand tools.

I've also done wrong, deliberately and remorselessly. In the past two years I ran up enormous credit card bills that I can't pay. Not the first time in life that I gambled with other people's money, a staple of filmed entertainment and artistic enterprise. I've been a cad with women repeatedly. These are real problems, primarily because I failed to produce much of anything in the world, if the measure of a man is his wallet. My wallet is empty. Women can take a lot of crap from their men, but being broke is unforgivable. Being bad tempered in defeat makes everything worse, so I make an effort to be cheerful. There is quite a lot to be happy about, so it's an authentic emotional response. I like being alive, enjoy the courage and joy of life in others, acknowledge and encourage work by talented friends and family.

However, I completely understand lone wolves — and I chose the pen name 'Wolf' in specific acknowledgment of my social demerit, a deplorable before it became fashionable. I was deeply influenced by Ayn Rand, an articulate exponent of selfishness. I took it seriously, saw life as a personal possession, mine to save or spend to the extent of my mental and physical ability, took no notice of what might be pragmatic, conservative, or pleasing to others.

Without asking anyone to agree with me, I believe that it is the human condition generally to be alone, fundamentally independent no matter how often or how deeply we congregate at work or play. I know that people derive pleasure from congress. Sporting events, religion and neighborhood gatherings are fun for all concerned, and I've seen pleasure in the workplace lots of times, although there's always a dollop of artificial enthusiasm. Work is called work for a reason. Given a choice, employees and supervisors would rather be somewhere else.

It's a special condition of privilege to be a loner, which is nearly impossible to maintain as an economic activity, unless one is particularly gifted. I know for a fact that I'm not exceptionally talented, except in the matter of selfhood. When I die, I doubt anyone will mourn. That's the price of selfhood as I understand it. Few people want such a fate. I do not recommend it as a life goal, unless you're an independent novelist or filmmaker, deaf and blind to pragmatism.

Marines

If you've ever met a Marine, any age, young or old, you know that they're a special breed — "devil dogs" and "jarheads," front line infantrymen who walk on water, fly close air support, fire mortars, take and hold real estate with their blood and guts, relentlessly fierce men who do the impossible. There are never enough Marines.

I don't doubt that there are brave men and women in every branch of military service. I have friends and relatives who served honorably and courageously on aircraft carriers, in armored divisions, logistics and supply, nuclear submarines. Missile silos and battlefield nukes are a frightful responsibility that cannot be dismissed lightly. We like to scoff at Pentagon waste, cosy procurement payola, and crazy red tape. That's not what Marines do. They are frontline infantry, insanely brave riflemen, bonded in brotherhood.

Not being a Marine, I made mistakes in writing (they don't have "medics," they borrow Navy corpsmen). Special forces like SEALs and Green Berets and Rangers are more numerous than Marine Raiders, a commando division that was disbanded long ago, recently reactivated to extend operations behind enemy lines.

I don't regret giving my fictional hero Chris Cable field rank as a Marine Corps officer, battle scars and emotional scars. He ordered men to their death and dismemberment, resigned his commission because he hated killing, having done so much of it. Officers need to be immune from emotion. My guy had a vulnerable soft spot, fought it down as a matter of discipline, to honor three generations of Marines and naval officers who gave him life, greased his officer candidacy and fast-track field promotions. He fought side by side with enlisted Marines, had no desire to shirk duty or danger.

But the killing was too much, far too much, a grisly butchery that Ivy League prep school did not predict or prepare him to metabolize.

So, he's a flawed Marine, unfit for flag rank, a disgrace in his father's eyes. No matter what he tries to do, the result is frustration. Couldn't abide the paperwork and fussy restraints of law enforcement. Licensed as a private investigator, he's a dangerous lone wolf that clients don't want to hire twice. I do this guy a favor, let him meet a woman whose courage, wealth, and brainpower propel them through three novels loaded with sex and violence. In honor of the great detective authors Ray Chandler and Dashiell Hammet, my stories are told first person, witnessing life and love and combat through Chris Cable's exceptionally warm blue eyes.

To be a Marine is to be part of a unit, fully integrated and bonded by team cohesion, a matter of doctrine, the source of Marine Corps power. Now imagine a Marine on his own, haunted by images of death and mutilation, much of it civilian casualties, battlefields red with blood — and the dishonor of resigning his commission as a decorated combat commander.

Interesting man, carries a 1911 and uses it. Semper Fi.

Musical honors and brickbats

I listen to classic rock when I write, a small number of FM stations in the Ozarks, although it's the same problem in major markets, too. Airhead disc jockeys play terrible rubbish over and over and over in rotation, while ignoring gems from the 60s, 70s, and 80s. I made a list of their high crimes and misdemeanors. The worst felony is a boycott of creativity, constantly plugging brainless junk by dunderheads like Allman, Osborne, Fogerty, and Boston.

Before I get to the YES, PLEASE and NO, NEVER playlists, I should say that I'm indifferent to the Stones, Bowie, Eagles, Arrowsmith, ZZ Top and a bunch of other defaults in the standard rotation. Zeppelin is properly hailed as a miracle of Bonham syncopation with outrageously brilliant Page and Plant, the only thing that classic FM does right when they air 'Black Dog' or 'The Ocean.' More Zep deep tracks would be swell, like 'The Rain Song' and 'Heartbreaker.' There was a big placard in the music department of a pawnshop in Golden, Colorado, stern warning to guitar and keyboard shoppers: NO STAIRWAY. Once a year is plenty, thanks.

However, there is a black list of awful crap that should be banished: Neil Young, Phil Collins, Fleetwood Mac and Stevie Nicks, Springsteen, U2, Dire Straits, Steely Dan, Guns & Roses, Blue Oyster Cult, Billy Joel, The Police, The B52s, Rush, Queen, and Elton John. Their digital files ought to be permanently destroyed with BleachBit as a public service to humanity.

Classic rock that I love will be explained in detail, starting with Blood Sweat & Tears. Few if any groups equalled the thrill of their showmanship, arrangements, and lyrical life on life's terms ('Spinning Wheel' and 'One Child Born to Carry On'). Jimi Hendrix is my next most favorite superstar, and he gets good airplay for a reason, whenever somebody sane is spinning the digital turntables. Ditto Jim Morrison, although they often play the wrong tracks. I'd much prefer to hear 'Roadhouse Blues' once in a while, please. Crissie Hynde is a marvel of modern womanhood, then and now and forever. She's a personal idol for good reason (she did TV show with me in London). Her Pretenders tracks 'Middle of The Road' and 'Talk To Me Darling' are far superior to 'Brass In Pocket', but I'd settle for more Chrissie, period. The other chick I'd like to hear more of is strumpy Benatar.

Next on my wish list is Zappa, although that has to be understood in context. Frank was more than a bad tempered joker. His repertoire included hard rock lampoon 'Fifty Fifty' for a reason. I don't care which tracks they play from HOT RATS, WAKA JAWAKA, APOSTROPHE, or OVERNIGHT SENSATION albums, it's all musical gold standard of orchestration and originality, doing what others could not begin to attempt. Frank was a composer who played guitar like no one else could, and his classic rock contemporaries knew it.

I'll breeze through the other groups I'd like to hear once in a while, please. ABBA had several tunes of brilliant musical structure and wonderful harmonies. Ditto the Wilson sisters (Heart) who made the standard rotation. Abba's melodic work inspired the Beejees, whose 'Nights On Broadway' belong on every FM playlist, instead of insanely stupid Michael Jackson.

Tell you what, I'll compromise. One play of monotonous, musically incompetent U2 for every three plays of Jethro Tull. No Pink Floyd or Van Halen, unless I hear Robert Palmer's 'Simply Irresistible.' I disbelieve that anyone wants to suffer smarmy McCartney or Harrison ever again. Maybe Tom Petty is gone for good reason, time to bury the jerk. If you want to resurrect real talent, spin King Crimson, Arthur Brown, or Dutch rocker Herman Brood.

Narcissism

I forget exactly how I became aware of it -- an online ad, I think -- that women were talking about narcissism, how men made life hell for everyone because they loved themselves and they wielded power accordingly, to the detriment of all concerned. Some men, the worst cases, are a constant drag psychologically and financially, because they are infatuated with themselves to the point of folly.

For 50 years I pursued the narcissistic business of creative work. Unlike reasonable men who applied themselves dutifully to economic endeavor, I was terrible at it, seldom worked at a paying job for long, and I threw myself into projects that failed because I wanted to do the unwanted. From time to time, less narcissistic people supported my self-absorbed "work."

As a matter of law and morality, my life was mine to spend, to go to hell in a handbasket if I chose. Now an old shell of a man without a job, a laughable resume consisting mainly of my hapless projects that died stillborn, I sympathize with men and women who were harmed, drawn by a magical nincompoop who offered nothing but self-absorbed bullshit. I'm trying to be honest about it. I cost friends and family several million dollars.

The problem of narcissism has narrowed during the last couple of years. I have undertaken to write literature of a sort that reflects antisocial values. The main character answers to no one, carries a gun and uses it recklessly — an action adventure hero in the tradition of James Bond and Philip Marlowe, men without social obligation. There are such men in reality. I've met them. They are cutthroats, spoiled sociopaths, criminals, and worthless heirs. I suppose that I qualify as all of the foregoing, certainly spoiled and coldly indifferent to debts owed to my bankers and credit card issuers who were cheated into extending a dime's worth of credit to me in the first place. Normal people don't do this. It doesn't make any sense, wreaks havoc, harms everyone in my orbit, especially wives and their children.

I can say these things because I like to be reality oriented, another aspect of self-love. What others do revulses me when they do work they hate, say things they cannot possibly believe are principled, except as a matter of survival. I was always a terrible employee, saw myself as an equal, a prince among men who were far richer and far more successful as human beings. It still puzzles me that so many can do the work of living without screwing it up, as I was wont to do, deaf to good counsel, blind to obvious conventions of society. Given a simple, ordinary job, I concocted bizarre projects and unwanted ideas, got tossed out on my ear after they'd had enough annoyance or embarrassment or both.

In the Objectivist canon, there is nothing to justify narcissism -- or art, for that matter, if you can call what I do artistic. Sometimes I regard my work as complete rubbish, poorly done, until someone hands me a book they enjoyed as fine literature. I have yet to read anything written by others that reflects my sense of story or style. That said, I was always generous to other writers of my acquaintance, saw virtue and value in their nonprofit ambitions without exaggerated flattery. I like artistic people. The bar of my approval is low, rather than high, unless their work is critically successful. I have a permanent resentment of the crap that New York and Hollywood pushes, not solely because I failed to win a lottery.

There were offers I refused as a director, not many but enough to sink my career. I would do amateur nonprofit work rather than studio ordained slasher movies and unfunny sitcoms. On small projects, I could be a prince among happy peasants. It did not improve my skills. It may be true of my writing as well. When one self-publishes ("vanity" publishing at bottom) there is no editor to point out screamingly obvious errors and ultimately regulate who is published and who is not. The vanity of narcissism is obvious. No books are sold.

If someone has worked at a career and saved for retirement, it is certainly their right to play with writing as a harmless pasttime, like sewing or craft projects involving styrofoam and pipe cleaners, growing tomatoes and peppers at a great cost of time and trouble. People earn the right to enjoy their Golden Years any way they please. I can't. I've saved nothing except myself. Arguably at retirement age and absolutely unemployable (trust me, I've tried) my days are spent consecutively, without interruption, writing tawdry novels that go unread and unsold, because it is the zenith of a lifelong ambition to succeed on terms I defined without consulting the neighbors. I live hand to mouth doing odd jobs as a laborer or carpenter.

There is little else to say about the matter of self-love. It's often the case that embarrassing failures teach one to wake the hell up and buckle down, buster, get on with earning money like everyone else, do the right thing. The emotional pressure of failure is horrid. I know it better than most people. However, I explained it to a friend recently as follows: I'm writing what I can write, gladly, but of necessity because I can do nowt else.

Natural rights hooey

My constitutional law professor repeated the same principle frequently, "An assertion is not an argument!" It was the only thing worth learning in law school. It is my unhappy duty to call your attention to a problem with natural rights. They are nothing but assertions. Mark Levin is full of shit. Rights are not bestowed by God.

Non-aggression doctrine is totally lame, asserting that all people everywhere are obligated to heed a kindergarten playground rule. It doesn't matter whether you conceive NAP as a political or ethical principle, utilitarianism, or The Golden Rule. NAP does not explain citizenship, marriage, custody, conservatorship, bankruptcy, property, or something as stupid as fake news told by people who believe it to be true. Socialists believe that all money and property are theirs to share, all children theirs to indoctrinate. Neo-cons believe that the defense of Israel justifies war on Iraq, Syria, Iran, Lebanon, and subjugation of Egypt under a military dictator. Billions of folks bow their heads in prayer on Friday (Islam) Saturday (Judaism) or Sunday (Christianity) and feel obligated to implant lunatic metaphysics in little children. Non-aggression feels more fair, but it has no teeth, no power to change the world, beyond an impotent plea to Live And Let Live. Tough guys like NAP because they feel justified in wreaking personal retribution for perceived or potential insult. Property is a slam dunk business of possession, according to "natural rights" monsters.

Government is another laughable assertion, whether by warlord, mafioso, or a show of hands in favor of free health care and exploration of Jupiter's moons. There is no natural right to form a conspiracy, a state, or a territorial border defended by police and military.

I like the supposition of individual rights, but there's a neighbor who doesn't agree with me. Now what? Assert that I'm right and he's wrong? Meanwhile, both of us have economic and national security interests at stake in a dangerous world. The Seventh Fleet has North Korea surrounded, ready to attack with thousands of aircraft, cruise missiles, and Marines. South Korean and Japanese forces are echeloned in a coordinated command structure, with B1-B strategic bombers on alert in Guam. On the other side of the world, our Fifth Fleet is ready to attack Iran, with Israel and Saudi Arabia clamoring to help us kill people and break things. In time of war, does national security trump personal rights? Government asserts that it does.

It's important to reflect that all of it — morality, military might, international treaties — are nothing more than artificial constructs reified by arbitrary assertions of will.

There is a rational alternative, buried under a mountain of historical misdirection, known as "the rule of law." It pains me to explain that it has nothing to do with the Declaration of 1776 or a Federal Union, no relation to Congress or state legislatures or county courthouses and jails. The rule of law is an objective principle to restrain contending foes, simply that "No man is entitled to judge his own cause." Common law cases are A vs B, both presumed innocent, each equally free to testify and submit evidence, to offer legal defenses and to argue points of law. Most cases are heard by a jury. The verdict must be unanimous. Jurors can be challenged for prejudice. The entire process of common law trial is driven by the notion of fundamental fairness. Prejudice (extralegal prejudgement) is verboten.

Huh? -- U.S. vs North Korea should be argued in court? Yep. But more importantly, the U.S. government is a "fictitious legal person." Any fair reading of U.S. history shows that we need to make changes, stop government from unilaterally crushing foreign and domestic foes. A good place to start is to free the judiciary from fealty to the state. At the Federal Convention of 1787, Ben Franklin proposed that private citizen lawyers should elect judges, because they would almost certainly elect the most successful of their number and, thus, divide amongst themselves his law clients. Judges are forbidden to practice law or to hear cases involving former law clients.

So, there's a free market solution (please, not "polycentric" or anything goofy like that).

I've written on the subject if you're interested in constitutional law. The Executive Branch is no different than an industrial project. It should be governed by company shareholders and subject to the rule of law. If we get our act together as a nation, perhaps there's hope for a future international court to adjudicate U.S. v Evil Foe — both sides heard by a jury, bloviating war talk ruled inadmissible as evidence. "They shouldn't have nuclear weapons!" will be the complaint. "Why not? -- you have them!" will be the rejoinder. Common law courts have a concurrent jurisdiction in equity, but law courts can't order anyone to disarm, unless they pose a clear and present danger to officers of the court or nearby civilians.

If I was sitting as a judge, I'd rule that there are other nations bordering Evil Foe -- it's *their* neighborhood to police -- and the United States is not a world cop. Go home and mind your own hemisphere.

Rule of law or unrestrained, unilateral dominance by the strong, take your pick.

Not notable

Easy to say, difficult to digest. I'm not notable. The term has specific meaning at Wikipedia. There is no Wikipedia article about Wolf DeVoon, and I very much doubt that my death will be noticed, except by the nice old lady who runs the general store. I owe a hefty balance.

My latest opus was issued in the size and shape of a child's coloring book, that's how little it mattered. Self-published books are invisible. I've written 23 of them. Web content doesn't count in terms of notability. I can't guess how many forum posts and blog posts I authored. Published magazine articles, radio interviews, and videos don't count, either. Wolf DeVoon won't be notable until SOMEONE ELSE decides to say something about me in the New York Times, Washington Post, Wall Street Journal, LA Times, Atlantic, New Yorker, Rolling Stone, GQ or Advertising Age. Colin Kapernik was celebrated by all of them, and he made the cover of Sports Illustrated, USA Today, and Time, despite being one of the worst quarterbacks in NFL history, eleven losses before he got fired for being incredibly stupid and vain.

Doesn't seem fair. I'm just as stupid, equally vain.

Politicians get noticed. Mass murderers and evangelists always get noticed. It's a coin toss whether a scientist might be notable, unless she's a guru of climate change and gender fluidity. Now that I think about it, it might be felony sexual harrassment to review a straight male novelist, universally shunned by agents and publishers. Chicks and queers rule the book trade.

I hit a million words recently, decades of effort, much of it writing full-time, because I have to have total solitude, months at a stretch to conceive and execute and polish something as huge as a novel.

I laugh about it some times. Facebook decided that I was a "public figure" with zero Likes and no Talking Abouts.

Breakfast, lunch, and dinner this week is discount balogna, slivers of onion, and mustard. I have one pack of cigarettes left, one pack of Ol' Roy soft food for my dog. He can't eat cheap kibble or defend himself because he lost half of his teeth to a lunatic vet. I lost half of mine over the years, so we're symmetrical, old and unable to do anything except to gum soft balogna and dream of boiled eggs, sharp cheddar, fried chicken, Dewar's on the rocks, hot rib eye.

Gracefully surrender the things of youth?

Okay, I suppose that my creative work was juvenile. I stood up for masculinity and gorgeous women, outlandish love stories in outer space and on the hot filthy streets of Los Angeles. I had them chase each other in Central Java and Oud Loosdrecht and Columbus Circle, places that were familiar to me, the plumes of another life, all six continents when I was young and handsome and daring. All that's left is daring to claim that what I wrote was important.

Not notable, just important.

Life, liberty, and the pursuit of justice.

Women

In previous writing, I quoted Mark Twain: "There is only one good sex, the female one." I argued that women should be exempt from the criminal law, given separate and equal share of government by constitutional amendment (the entire House of Representatives) and a monopoly of civilian law enforcement. It is my conviction that women have a separate moral purpose apart from men, one which a man learns to understand in marriage but never fully embraces because it would unman him.

Generally speaking, always foolish to do so, women as a species are resolute, industrious, coy, secretive, curious and observant. When she gives birth, she is "settled" and her primary purpose sharpens to an absolute, amplifying her powers. Above all, motherhood confers the will to kill, a fierce adjudicator of life and death, if man or beast threatens her cubs.

No different than men in some respects, women can be self-destructive (drug addiction and alcoholism, prostitution, thievery, and irrational tantrums). The human condition applies to both sexes equally, but women have a deep silence and arbitrariness that men often see as disturbing and mysterious. She can smile come hither then sneer go to hell unpredictably.

In Rescuing Flopsie, it was imperative to depict women as individuals, some ideal, some ordinary, and one seriously deranged and murderous, none of which are typical. The purpose of fiction is to offer contrasts, danger, intrigue, combat, and the costly price of triumph. Only the most admirable of women will undertake a mission of steely commitment separate from a biological and utilitarian destiny that urges her to play along, suffer a load of shit without response.

Men do it, too. They knuckle under to keep a job, obey the laws and customs of polite society, shun risk of a painful adventure with uncertain outcome. Warriors are few.

There have been numerous heroic female warriors -- Boadicea, Joan of Arc, Phoolan Devi, Emiline Pankhurst, and Margaret Thatcher spring to mind, but there were many thousands in world history. If I was a better student, I would remember more names, like the wildcat who disarmed and stood on the neck of an invader that she would come to admire and mate as his queen. Every student should know the steadfastness and courage of Marie Curie and Florence Nightingale, the charismatic crusades of Aimie Semple McPherson, Mary Baker Eddy, Susan B. Anthony, Madame Blavatsky, Ayn Rand, Gloria Steinem, and Anne Coulter.

Women dominate literature for good reason, because women read. They play second fiddle to movie heroes and villains, but without women on screen there is very little story to tell, merely men struggling to kill each other. One of the best classic films is *The Inn of The Sixth Happiness* starring Ingrid Bergman, the true story of an English housemaid who decided that her mission in life was to go to China and preach the Gospel, traveling alone on the Trans Siberian Railway and by ox cart, given official status to abolish the cruelty of foot binding and, amid the horror and destruction of a Japanese invasion, to rescue 150 orphan children by leading them hundreds of hours through the mountains. Women do these things because they are biologically impelled to save life and ameliorate suffering. In American colonial history and medieval Europe, women were the healers and heretics that men feared and persecuted, then banished or killed and slandered in bitter calumny.

I owe a great deal to Ayn Rand in particular, a woman who stood alone, did whatever she had to, and fought for the right to be heard. In the beginning, she was awkward and inarticulate. Her ideas of good and evil, true and false and logically necessary took Rand decades to refine and express in English, concepts that were forged by experiencing Soviet Russia as a young adult. I could not have learned to think clearly without Rand's compelling achievement. She paid an incredibly high price, shunned and betrayed and villified.

That said, my style of storytelling has nothing to do with Ayn Rand's example, although her novels mesmerized me and taught me about passion, notably absent from male authors like Dashiell Hammett and Raymond Chandler. It's amusing and revealing that Rand liked Mickey Spillane's Mike Hammer and Ian Fleming's James Bond, hard men of action. Her own fictional male heroes were intelligent, upright, unbending, creative, courageous, and virile.

I'm a little different. My hero is sufficiently valiant but slightly stupid, as most men are. His principal virtue is a sort of plodding endurance, instilled by Marine Corps discipline, always faithful and inured to hardship and danger. The woman he met and married was in a class by herself, spectacularly alert, bisexual, a polymath with a Ph.D. -- genius level brilliant -- the elder daughter of a billionaire inventor, a father she despised. Her younger sister is a brat, twisted by fear and seething monstrosity, as ugly and vicious as a woman could be.

To inhabit their femininity, their female physiology and biorhythms, was a daunting task as a male novelist. Like my hero Chris Cable, I'm slightly stupid, attempted the clumsy heresy of writing a female point of view told in first person.

A woman's life is enormous. Think of it exactly so, as massive as an egg, with millions of tiny aggressive sperm vying to penetrate and spawn new life, only one of which can succeed, a primeval right to choose under assault, the result of reflexive or involuntary union. What will happen next will forever transform her, unless she elects to remain childless by employing a foolproof method of birth control like having her tubes tied, a decision to live for her own sake as a high priestess, independent of biological destiny. More than ever before in history, fertile young women are drawn to a career and a personal crusade, the hunt for an equal to love and honor, uncomplicated by the duty of children. Others want very much to breed and nurture, gift themselves in service to the future, hoping that men will protect them.

Men are untrustworthy in that regard, however much they enjoy the warmth and wonder of innocence. That's why an exceptional class of female warrior must step into the fray and kick with the strength of her kind, indifferent and hardened to men and women alike, unless they share an equal dedication to justice, the armed defense of cherished liberty, bulwark of our nation's commerce, energy production, farms and factories to feed and clothe children.

One last birthday

I have the notion that I'm dying, no particular reason for it, a general sense of frailty. In two weeks I will be 68 years old. The last thing I want to do is shiver through another winter, and I don't see much purpose in doing that. How did old indians die? — walk into a frozen cave, lay down and die. Better than suffering in a hospital bed, plaything for medical experiments that never work, bombarded by television. I can't think of a worse hell, inescapable TV made by evil shitheads. Maybe that's what mythological hell is like, tormented by the obscene, a long wicked laugh at my expense. Memo to Lucifer: it won't work, bub. I don't care what you or anyone else throw at me. I've been ridiculed plenty, no stranger to verbal punishment. Try physical torture.

I have to get in line with reality. No one will ever find my work, buried under a mountain of horseshit on the web, millions of people in universities pushing conventional wisdom. If you want to honor my death, play Led Zeppelin's 'When The Levee Breaks.' It propelled my first novel, listened to it looped endlessly while I wrote the action scenes. Make a note (hat tip to Alejandro): music first, then story.

Another note. Talented people are generous. I don't know that I include myself in that class, but maybe I am, always generous with other writers and filmmakers similarly situated, good work that didn't stand a micron of hope to be recognized or rewarded by the Jews. Sorry to be offensively blunt. Look around, follow the money in publishing, movies, music, stage. Drunk or sober, Mel had it right. Nice that I shared dinner and lunch the next day with him, a great guy. Not the best actor on Earth, certainly not a director, just a wonderful man with plenty of women and children. I understood him. I lost track of how many women and children I had.

Someday someone will write a nice biography of Mel Gibson. That's the difference between him and me. When I die, everything I did will die with me, unacknowledged.

The world keeps secrets. Sigh. Too many to discuss. Obama's school records are sealed for a reason. Hillary destroyed emails for a reason. The Civil War had nothing to do with slavery. The U.S. Constitution had little to do with deliberate rational design.

Hmph. This wasn't supposed to be a political screed, damn it. I wanted to wish myself a last happy birthday greeting. Dead certain that no one else will. There is a wife and daughter up the hill who will ignore September 30th, dissing Dad for the thousandth time. People indulge bad habits to make themselves feel superior. My bad habits are slightly different. I smoke pot to see visions, feel the beat of life; cigarettes to kill the pain of loneliness.

I think I've covered everything in essays and in autobiographical stories, clips and stills in a five minute salute to myself. Happy birthday, Dorf. Long way from juvenality to Wolf DeVoon. It could have been far worse, a machinist's apprentice or factory hand.

Bye, Clare.

Physical work

Physical work saves me. A tall dead red elm crashed in the last storm, crumpled a cow panel and wrecked the gate I built. Yesterday the trunk and big limbs got bucked with a chain saw, enough to clear the wreckage, so I could repair the gate. Hauled four wheelbarrows of dry wood rounds to the concrete pad behind the wood barn, piled them high on top of another cord of windfall, two thirds of which was a huge oak struck by lightning and felled by the power utility, because it might hit a pole if it fell uncontrolled. Just now I gathered brush, hauled it to the burn pile, six trips like the huntsman in Snow White, armloads of twisted branches. My women flip out in a panic whenever I light a burn pile, eight feet around and almost as high, the flames shooting up 40 feet for a few minutes, then a long hot burn as it collapses. I get yelled at and I patiently point to the evidence. See? Didn't get away from me. I stood by with jugs of water and a shovel. Nothing but flat cold ashes on a calm green day.

Last week, I installed heavy 5/8" sheetrock on the ceilings of an old farmhouse bathroom and front porch with room dimensions and rafters that were wacky, nothing square or uniformly spaced. The rock weighed a ton, had to keep it braced with one hand and the top of my head, fumble for a screw gun on the ladder, dropped dozens of screws. Exhausting work for hire, sore for days.

It saves me, like the sound of thunder and hailstones battering my writing office, doing fun notes like this one. Whenever I complete a chapter of 'Partners' I'm so upset with a dramatic finish that I have to go out and do physical work, split wood with a mawl, pick up the string trimmer and whack an acre or two, take a hand saw to the sycamore and stop it from growing into a 7000 volt high line. Insistent nature is always victorious, unless you fight it. We have bears, coyotes, cougars, and meth head trailer trash in beat up wrecks on the county road that bisects our property. There's a rifle with a scope next to the front door.

Anything is good, an excuse to get up from the keyboard, forget if I can. The story follows me wherever I go, scanning the ground for rattlesnake and copperhead, worn work gloves on my hands. I forgive myself, try to focus on physical reality, avoid injuries. Small and old, I have to work slowly. The wild calm grandeur of nature is sedative.

To begin a new chapter is so daunting a task that it takes days to conceive, test driving ideas. It takes forever to see the solution, always a notch higher and deeper. Stories cannot go in reverse or tread water. Characters do not become simpler, unless they die. I'm in the habit now of quoting an epigram from a literary source on the title page. In 'Finding Flopsie' I recited Scott Fitzgerald to introduce Chris's story, O. Henry for The Way Peachy Saw It. The venerated opener for 'Partners' was Jim Morrison: "The future's uncertain, and the end is always near." Oh, but not near enough, miles to go before I finish. Tense miles uphill.

Not just the present business of writing 'Partners,' a particularly challenging endeavor, but writing as such, each page a little more difficult because I keep aiming higher. Whether that succeeds or fails is less important. Novelists do not become simpler unless they die.

The dog helps. Always something to do, food, water, trim endlessly with a scissors, flea baths and tick removal. He's hilarious, too old and shrewd to be tricked. Doesn't even look up when I call him. He has general store privileges, lays on the floor on Wednesdays when folks come to sit and swap gossip at the tables in back. I throw horseshoes in the shade of a walnut tree outside, try to hold my own with a crew of old faces, ignore their protestations of frustration and watch them toss double ringers. Three or four hours away from writing, a lifeline.

If all else fails, there's Solitaire, a 3% chance of winning. I play from 5 to 7 in the evening, eat something and listen to vain asshole Mark Levin pat himself on the back. After eight hours of writing, I need to quit, wrung out and creatively drained. Talented people don't have these problems.

Springsteen

If I'm so smart, how come I'm not rich? I listen to classic rock in the mornings while I write (maybe that's the problem) and I just got disgusted for the umpteenth time by Springsteen's "Glory Days," a stupid song shouted by an empty-headed dolt, musically dull and repetitive. Made me think of the idiotic bullshit of Top 40 when I was a kid, until the Beatles and Stones shattered the monopoly of Tin Pan Alley crap and forced them to cough up bigger stuff than doo-wop and Dino, with new fakirs like Barry Manilow pretending to woo fat ladies.

The cabal never quits. Incapable of topping Jimmy Page, they fought back with filthy rotters like Phil Collins and tinsel queen Elton John, then the vile hell of gangsta rap. The cabal is a spiritual serial killer, no room in their inn for anything decent or sane. Our newspaper carries USA Today as a daily supplement, color front page obscenity today plumping Christmas Past — Bruce Willis in DIE HARD and shithead Bill Murray's SCROOGED from 1988, BATMAN RETURNS (1992), and KRAMPUS (2015) in which a boy who has a bad Christmas summons a demon.

On page two, AP praised the cabal's latest hardcovers. Ready? "The Man in the Crooked Hat" is about grief and what-ifs. "The Whispering Room" is a conspiracy to brainwash people, force them to commit horrific acts. A schoolteacher sets her car on fire and drives through a hotel lobby. "Artemis" celebrates a chick who shuns work, gets suckered by money. "End Game" does away with a covert ops boss, sends two star-crossed lovers to find out what happened to him in a small Colorado town. The hero can't understand why his partner is frigid.

I must be stupid. Anyone can make moolah. It ain't difficult. They told me how to do it in Hollywood, repeatedly. Change your name, marry a Jewish girl, and convert. Take marching orders from a fat uncle, schmooze, and watch what sells. Not joking. People tried to help me when I was young and cute. Now it's too late, because I became Wolf DeVoon, a creature of my own making, deeply revulsed by trash, everything that Bruce Springsteen and his management are not.

All together now! Jerusalem is the capital of Israel, always was.

The good of the nation

I forget -- oh! -- now I remember. Wilda's lede in her weekly gossip column suggested doing something for The Good Of The Nation, which seemed like common sense to heed. I told her I'd get right on it, patted her affectionately and came home to my writer's lair, if you can call a tin barn a writer's lair. It has a coffee pot, microwave, laptop, and a plywood bunk that needs a pillow. The old one became so filthy with mold that I had to toss it on a flaming brush pile, along with that week's trash bags. I generate a lot of garbage, not exactly good for the nation, but it's life on life's terms in rural living. A year ago when I still had a car, I drove trash bags to town and let the town garbage collectors bury or burn it. If I understand the national situation correctly, every consumer in the United States produces tons of waste.

Nothing I can do about that. Voting won't fix it. Same intractable problem with 9,220 Veterans Administration buildings and 49,000 Dept. of Agriculture offices and inspection stations, plus 373,000 miles of road maintained by the Forest Service, a USDA subsidiary. The military? Hah. Defense occupies 696,470 buildings worldwide, plus 8 million square feet in Virginia. Roughly six million people are directly or indirectly employed by the Pentagon, not including allies. In the Old World, allies were called "auxilliaries," had to be fed and watered, disinclined to do much serious fighting, unless they were British Gherkas. Ancient history. War is a Raytheon inventory to be launched by stealth fighter or drone nowadays. There's not much that you or I or anyone else can do to enhance national security. It's already the third-largest budget item funded by government, after Social Security and Medicare. I'm not sure that anything can be done to assist the Corps of Engineers with 650 dams, 12,000 miles of channel, and 926 harbors to maintain.

I'm not big on voting. The last time I voted was in 2008, because Sarah Palin was on the ticket, a reasonably normal person, guileless and honest. Since then I spent quite a lot of time at my laptop, exercising my remaining wit, hoping to contribute inspirational literature for The Good Of The Nation.

I should have stood in bed, as the expression goes. Jews, blacks, gays, and doe-eyed victims of Christianity have a lock on publishing and the 16x9 public square of televised squabbling. Frozen out, I self-published twenty books. Good joke on me. A decade of effort exiled my work to laughable obscurity. My latest and best novel was shunted to Amazon.mx, denied existence in English, deemed unfit for American readers. Mighty hard to leverage The Good Of The Nation when the nation in question forbids new entrants to the marketplace of ideas.

"Free speech has limits," they scold. "You can't shout fire! in a crowded theater."

Maybe that was my mistake, I should have shouted fire in a gay nightclub, won a customary fifteen minutes of fame as a patriotic pariah, a noodlemeyer paraded in an orange jumpsuit and leg irons. If I owned a car, I could have waved a tiki torch in Charlottesville, shaved what little hair I have left on my head. Unfortunately, I don't give a shit about Confederate statues or any other legacy writ in concrete. The focus of my work was liberty, an extinct species of civil rights, and embarrassingly frank cis-het adventure novels, an antique artform.

It seems strange that national progress should be left in the care of bartender Sean Hannity and butch Rachel Maddow, but they're certainly less boring than Andy Rooney was, energetic binaural eclipse of monotone Sunday night CBS schtick. I give Fox and MSNBC a one finger digital salute and note in passing the fan-losing Negro Football League taking a suicidal knee for The Good Of The Autonomous Vehicle Gig Economy Queer Nation.

Mom always said that I was an optimist. Liberty is the future for some of us, unwilling to bend over for modernity.

Conveyances

It's been an interesting life.

All sorts of cars and trucks, a fire engine, an ambulance, a bulldozer, and a betjah. Hovercraft, ferries of all sizes, outboards, rafts, the Queen Mary, a canal barge, DC-8, DC-9, 707, 727, 737, Trident, Fokker, L-1011, 747, 757, 767, 777, Airbus, Embreaer, and BAE. An ancient prop with magneto ignition, a fast Cessna turboprop, an ultralight, ATV, utility crane, go cart, sled, and horseback. A wheelchair, a Chapman, a doorway dolly, shopping cart, and handheld leaning out of a TR-3. The parlor car on the 20th Century Limited, dining car on the Hiawatha, and the rung of a freight car. Subways, buses, British Rail, moving sidewalks, steam trains, a surgical gurney, and a parade float. Memorable taxi rides, golf carts, and Town Cars. Thousands of elevator doors opening and closing, an infinity of stairs, escalators, cobbles, asphalt, gravel, concrete, cornfields, storm drains, white sand beaches, ladders, and a bicycle built for two. My favorite destination was rural Luxembourg, but Singapore was pretty damn splendid.

If I was granted a wish, Elko beckons.

Curses, foiled again

Well, hell. I didn't die in my sleep and I had a bunch of weird dreams. I convinced Nancy Pelosi to allow me to make a movie during her Parade of Triumph with two thousand nicely dressed middle class victims on a nice summer day. I improvised a bunch of silly scenes with amateurs who agreed to do Fellini-style comedy gags, and when I pushed an elevator button in a hotel, the door was opened by a prosperous Jewish lawyer and his girlfriend. It wasn't an elevator, it was his apartment. I apologized, explained the mistake and persuaded him to produce the movie. I demonstrated why it would cost $5000, visualizing a mile-long strip of 16mm that had to be edited. He seemed intrigued, so I went to get my 3rd wife and her boyfriend, all of us penniless, said we were going to see a movie at a theater somewhere in London which always confuses me because it's in the future and twice as big and twice as poor as present. I told them to sit in a restaurant, I'd be right back after I found the cinema.

Sure enough, I was on the wrong street, no movie house. Then the dog started barking on his chain outside and NPR was broadcasting choral crap (in reality). I was awake and went out to discover that my 4th wife's stupid dog was at the door, had raided my shihtzu's food bowl again, and was happy to see me (in reality). I yelled at her and told her to go home. Another day with nothing to do, another morning to blow my nose, cough, wash my face, brush my teeth, smoke cigarettes and eat Oscar Mayer when I think I'm ready to deal with it again.

Maybe I'll ford the creek on foot and walk a mile and a half to Carol's house, move a log that's blocking a spot in the forest where she wants to park her truck, the solenoid of which had finally been fixed by a shade tree mechanic after a two month delay for no reason.

Yesterday, I waited four hours to do carpentry without doing any, while my dysfunctional clients, a brother and sister, quarreled with each other. I declined the opportunity to eat a splendid chicken dinner with them and walked home in the dark to liberate my dog. I had left him locked in the tin barn for his own safety. We have owls as big as flying elephants, packs of hungry coyotes on the hunt for fluffy little shihtzus.

Scanning my eight available FM channels in the barn, Janet Mefford called Donald Trump a disrupter-in-chief, hurrying the End Times. Reminded me of an AFR interview with a writer who was visiting Saudi Arabia, had sold 10 million copies in a popular series of novels about the End Times. Very respectable, calm and confident about his place in the world. I switched to a Salem broadcast hosted by Eric Metaxas. His guest explained that, despite the doctrine that Jesus was descended from King David, Joseph wasn't his biological father. God was.

Excuse me. I have to trim my shihtzu's feathers. They grow and grow and grow, and I have to scissor some matted tangles between his legs, not something he's pleased to let me do.

Dear Rush

I think you're capable of understanding, so I'll lay it out in simple terms. There is no divine right of incorporation. Voting doesn't change that. Exhorting folks to vote differently will not change it. People always vote their wallets. Fifty percent of workers are directly or indirectly employed by Federal, state, local, utility and school district governments — all of which are "fictitious legal persons," no different than corporations. The unemployed get free food and medicine from government. Social Security and Medicare recipients are paid far more than they paid in. Medicaid is a free ride for every wetback and anchor baby, every heroin addict, meth head, gang banger, and their SNAP sucking extended families, who are motivated to vote more unearned "rights" supported by taxation -- free lawyers, frivolous appeals, prison doctors, food, exercise, education, charity, and parole supervision, unless they're deported at taxpayer expense to repeat the whole idiotic cycle of catch and release again.

U.S. military veterans atone for killing foreigners by milking us twice, lifetime benefits and public salutes. Remind me, please, what's the purpose of exploring Jupiter's moons, landing another robot on Mars, or sailing past Pluto? How many millions of children get free breakfast, lunch, and dinner served by schools that do not and cannot discipline or educate them?

There's no easier path to power than being born black, becoming a community organizer, a teacher, a pro athlete, a must-hire academic, a paper pusher enforcing affirmative action, or an ugly thug chanting rap. Jews don't have the problem of community organizing. Jews own you, them, and us. Jews don't worry about skyrocketing drug deaths, homelessness, suicides, migrant caravans, pot consumption, gaming, pornography, binge viewing, or social media — fatal goy dissipations that are cash flow positive for Jewish bankers and media barons.

How is it our permanent duty to guarantee the security of Israel? Japan? Korea? We support dictators and Islamic honor killing in Saudi Arabia, Egypt, Pakistan and Afghanistan, throw big bucks at corrupt Haiti, Iraq, Columbia, Mexico, Uganda, and South Sudan. We have troops in 120 countries, 3.4 billion square feet of Federal government structures, plus 230,000 state and local offices, schools, hospitals, jails, and higher ed lecture halls. Total national public debt is never discussed. States, localities, and their utilities owe nearly as much as the Federal folly, measured in tens of trillions, with hundreds of trillions in unfunded obligations. If interest rates were allowed to float to an historic average, say 4%, it would kill leveraged con artists from sea to shining sea, halt shale drilling, mortgage lending and construction. We're paying farmers not to farm, bureaucrats to party in Vegas, students to stop free speech, and TSA to paw infants, cute chicks, and frail white grandmothers. FBI field agents reported that Saudi diplomats financed Saudi commandos who trained to fly jets in Florida, and did nothing to stop them. Russia warned the FBI about the Tsarnaev brothers. They were interviewed and cleared, no different than the Orlando gay nightclub jihadi. Comey and Mueller had much more important work to do, protecting the Clintons.

Face it. All of it, every bit of it, was the handiwork of democracy. There was no definition of justice provided in our allegedly sacred corporate charter repeatedly amended by legislation and judicial fiat. In the Legal Tender Cases over a century ago, common law was burned and buried, so that legislators could do whatever they pleased, and they were pleased to rob their neighbors' purses, to hand out loot that they did not earn, and to pledge more theft in the future to satisfy foreign lenders and future entitlement beneficiaries, perpetuating a preposterous ponzi racket, stage managed by Goldman alumni and K Street lobbyists.

There is no divine right of incorporation, certainly not as a carnival sideshow led by crooks and liars. If I was Donald Trump, I'd say to hell with it and quit.

I'll ghostwrite a resignation tweet: "It was stupid to reelect evil rats like Pelosi and Schumer. You're fired, America."

I appreciate that you've achieved a lot. I listened to your radio show since the 80s, watched your short-lived TV show, and I'm okay with your trademark bombast about "talent on loan from God" and "excellence in broadcasting." Arguably, the Tea Party could not have come into being without dittoheads, although it was Rick Santori who kicked it off. A lot of folks were players, especially Roger, right?

Too little, too late. We went to hell on 9/11.

Big surprise, huh? Cantor Fitzgerald was targeted. Nobody asked why. The secret Cheney Energy Commission had already chosen Iraq as a strategic plum, and it was easy to convince dumbshit George W. to blame Saddam, our former ally given battlefield chemical weapons. Mossad ginned up "evidence" of yellowcake and aluminum tubes. No curiosity why Exxon and Halliburton needed Iraqi oil, or why Saddam had invaded Kuwait because they were drilling horizontally, or why Arab clerics led commandos to attack Cantor Fitzgerald twice, starting with the garage bombing in 1993, payback for Harry Truman's creation of Israel and deployment of American power to defend legally indefensible Zionist conquest of Palestine. The successful Islamic revolution led by Khomeni proved that American oil companies could be ejected and CIA "royal" pawns dethroned.

Look, I understand entertainment, especially comedy. You had a winning package, hilarity and jingoism, snarky sarcasm and triumphal flag-waving patriotism. It made you rich and famous, an asset to the entrenched ruling class in Houston. Swell for you, sewing together evangelical Born Again boobs and easily-led boomers who wanted government off their backs and out of their bedrooms. Care to explain how Obama won two terms and killed the health insurance industry, ignited race riots, and launched a murderous Arab Spring?

You, more than anyone else, were personally responsible for the murder of millions, waste of trillions in Iraq and Afghanistan, chaotic tomfoolery that destroyed the Republican Party, and the meteoric rise of populist savior Donald Trump.

Happy about it, that Trump beat Cinton? It's about to explode, another Limbaugh laugh riot gone rotten, excellence in cheap entertainment, playing pattycake with a battered white middle class who think that a bankrupt corporate sovereign and comedy will make them prosperous and safe again.

It won't and can't.

Has it occurred to anyone?

Has it occurred to anyone that the government shutdown should be made permanent?

If I understand it correctly, essential services are uninterrupted, Social Security and Medicare payments continue to gush, the Treasury is borrowing and jawboning as usual, and DoD has about a million people stationed all over the world eating three squares. FBI, DEA, and BATF are staffed 100%, and there's no question that Capitol Police and Secret Service are being paid. The Federal Government is the world's largest consumer of gasoline, diesel, and jet fuel, paying up to $100 a gallon to deliver it to Afghanistan. All of our MRAPs, F-16s, and ships at sea are still in business, every tank truck, barge, and escort.

It's hard to grasp how big the government is. Nine hundred thousand structures around the world, 3.4 billion square feet, 122 square miles under roof, with over two million vehicles and aircraft parked outside. Estimates of Federal employees and contractors are between thirty and fifty million, depending on how you count teachers, college professors, coaches, doctors, bankers and brokers worldwide who skim a six-figure income from Treasury debt, mortgage scalpers underwritten by Fannie, Freddie, Ginnie, FHA, and Section 8 largesse.

It's dead certain that Boeing, General Dynamics, and Raytheon would collapse without fat DoD contracts, but their national defense cash flow is contractual, immune from shutdown. If I had to wager, I'd bet that Congressional staff and travel junkets are immune, too.

I trust you know that the Government annually spend a trillion or so more than it takes in from taxes and an infinity of fees including tariffs, asset seizures, and fines. The Feds are roughly $22 trillion in debt, unless you count unfunded entitlements of $200+ trillion. So, the obvious question is: why not make this temporary 25% shutdown permanent? It won't balance the budget or nick the ever expanding entitlement gravy train, but it's a nice down payment.

Oooo, scary. People out of work!

I don't see why not. Every dollar the government spends on itself is a dollar taken from the private free enterprise economy, engine of all innovation and profit, minus the burden of regulatory compliance and shipping and handling by tax accountants and molasses slow bureaucrats who can't be fired or compelled to show up for work.

Returning medical practice to the doctors would be nice. When I was a young man, we paid doctors in cash like plumbers and grocers. All private hospitals did charity cases, no charge. I know it's hard to believe, but drugs were cheap. Not in some distant prehistoric time, but in the 1960s, before affordable Blue Cross was hijacked by a tidal wave of suddenly sacrosanct welfare payola, illegal aliens, and anchor babies.

I'd like to see Congress undertake a new mission, no new laws, only repeals, but I'll take a 25% shutdown gladly. Let it run a few months. Kick the tires on smaller government. Make it easier to hire people in the private sector by cutting regulations — or the furlough enforcement staff, turn off a few light bulbs and computer screens, have a garage sale and sell off some of the quarter million GSA vehicles that regulators toodle around in. It'll be difficult to retrain former government employees to do anything efficiently and cheerfully, but newspapers say that there are more jobs available than those unemployed, so a big chunk of the 800,000 out of work at Federal agencies will be snapped up in a hurry by private employers. Who knows? They might enjoy working for a living, instead of snoozing at the Bureau of Paperwork.

I'm told by NPR that vital Homeland Security operations like TSA are working without being paid. First off, pull the plug on NPR, thanks. TSA should be funded by airlines and airports and ordered to keep their hands off frequent flyers, cute chicks, grannies, and children.

Above all, bring the troops home. Not just a handful from Syria. An orderly retreat from bases in Korea, Okinawa, Guam, Bahrain, Kuwait, Afghanistan, Germany, and Saudi Arabia would go a long way toward enhancing national security, concentrating on defense of North America, patrolling our shores and borders. International trade is a stupid justification for imperialism, and there's no sane purpose attempting to police the Islamic world as badly as we police Chicago.

Whether private citizens want to subsidize Israel or cancer research is up to them. Voluntary associations are the whole meaning of a free society. Let freedom ring and put the Federal government on a Weight Watchers diet, shed some bloated trillion dollar deficits.

* * *

UPDATE: I've been laughing my ass off, listening to NPR interview bureaucrats furloughed from EEOC and NASA climate change agitprop, claiming to be patriotic public servants who can't make ends meet on six-figure salaries and temporary loss of one paycheck.

Worse, dumbshit conservative radio talk host Mike Gallagher, after a visit to the White House, bitched that he couldn't buy a pair of Trump cufflinks at the Executive Office Building Gift Shop, closed because of the government shutdown.

Just take me away

I'm not ungrateful for the gift of life, nor the possibility of success some day in the distant future, but I'd much rather pass away quietly in my sleep tonight. It's been too long a wait to be discovered and rewarded, too miserable and frustrating to deal with another cold night, nothing recognizably sane on the BBC. No car, no phone, no internet, no cash.

I cough 1000 times a day, maybe more. If I lay on my left side, it wracks and chokes, gasping for air. I run through tissues like an army of rats building a Kleenex city, three boxes a week, a costly expense item second to dog food for my shihztu and cigarettes. Vaguely human vittles for me comes third, Oscar Mayer and stale bread for breakfast, lunch and dinner seven days a week. I had to punch two new holes in my belt. Never any chicken, no orange or cranberry or grapefruit juice, no eggs or hamburger or cornflakes or pizza. Prisoners have a better diet. I cut my own hair with a scissors, looking in a plastic mirror.

I can't kill myself, because I don't want my daughter to suffer that. It has to be something as polite as stroke or heart failure.

There's nothing further to write after eight novels, a dozen nonfiction books, two decades of forum posts, essays, short stories and screenplays, a new theory of justice and a constitution, video lectures and radio interviews, a long trail of work-for-hire in print, original work on film and pro tape. No man has had more opportunity to be heard or less recognition. I shouldn't complain. Two pals gave me flattering book reviews last year. Amazon paid me $24. I earned five hundred doing carpentry and day labor. Nice neighbors gave me an old jacket and rubber boots to ford the creek after a drenching thunderstorm.

I can't remember the last time I sat in a restaurant, slept on clean sheets in a hotel room, used a credit card to buy gasoline, a Coke, or an airline ticket. I'm ready to die.

There's a tombstone web page that a friend hosted yesterday.

wolfdevoon.net